The Black

H. Hofmann: Country wedding at the turn of the century

A travel guide to all parts
of the Black Forest, with
numerous maps and town plans

Text: Joachim Ott, Emmendingen

Table of Contents

The Black Forest

The Black Forest is bounded on its southern edge by the upper Rhine and on its northern edge by the Kraichgau plain on the east bank of the Rhine, a total length of about 160 kilometres. The western edge of this mountainous area, probably the best-known of all in Germany, is formed by the Rhine rift valley, and 30 to 50 kilometres away its eastern slopes peter out into the Baar, the plateau separating it from the hills of the Swabian Alb, or run down into the upper Neckar valley.

From south to north, from east to west, the Black Forest changes its countenance. Whereas the landscape in the southern half is dominated by rounded peaks and the interplay of wooded heights and broad vistas of open valleys, in the northern part it consists of wooded hills and open uplands.

Even nowadays it is easy to follow the life-history of the Black Forest by simply looking at a map. About 60 million years ago, the Earth formed a vaulted ridge running from south to north along a tectonic fault which ran across Europe. The present-day region of the Upper Rhine, the Black Forest, and the Vosges mountains on the French side was forced upwards several thousand metres over a period of innumerable years, together with the layers of stone on top of them.

Along the top of this vault, the Earth's crust started to crack. The result is the symmetrical trench of the Rhine rift valley dividing the "sister-hills" of the Black Forest and the Vosges. In the south, where this upward movement was at its strongest, are the highest peaks: Feldberg and Belchen on the German side, and the "Ballons" of Alsace on the French side. Erosion of the stone layers, which varied in their degrees of hardness, formed the present-day landscape with its typical flat layers and steep "steps", a striking feature all the way from the upper Rhine to the Swabian Alb.

One of the delights of travelling through the Black Forest is the interplay of landscape and climate. On the upper Rhine plain, mild air streams up from the south-west through the Burgundy Gateway, and even the upper Rhine foothills demonstrate this favourable climate with their vineyards and orchards. At the higher levels of the Black Forest, however, which block the passage of these westerly air streams, the clouds tip out their wet loads, and the lower temperature at these heights turn the rain into snow - to the delight of the winter-sports fans. Human beings evidently found this natural area delightful more than 2,000 years ago, but in those days perhaps more for its resources than its beauty. The Black Forest was settled by Celtic tribes as long ago as the 5th century BC. Romans mingled with them from the 1st century BC onwards, and gave the region its name silva nigra, from the much denser forests of those days.

The thermal baths are by far the most striking legacy the Romans left behind. These warm springs were also a guiding factor in the settlements of the Alemannic tribes that followed the Romans nearly 1,000 years later. It was not until about 1,000 AD that people started systematically clearing the Black Forest and creating settlements in the clearings. Monasteries formed the first islands of settlement, and the land around them was gradually tamed. The most important source of energy was water, and the main raw material was wood. Along the Rivers Neckar and Enz, via Murg and Nagold, the wood was sent in the form of might rafts to Holland, where it was used for ship-building. Charcoal-burners also used wood for their craft, and mines were dug to extract ore.

The density of the settlements increased in the 12th century, which was dominated mainly by the rulers of the Zähringen dynasty. They established towns and built castles, and the area of the Black Forest was an important power factor in the disputes with the Staufen monarchs over the Swabian Duchy. When the Zähringen line died out in the 13th century, a territory broke to pieces that had previously been extraordinarily self-contained. After that, the Margraves of Baden and also the western Austrian Habsburgers contributed to its disintegration, and the effects can still be seen today, for instance in the different strengths of the various religious confessions.

Black Forest people were subjected to another trial of strength after the second world war, when a referendum was held to determine whether the Swabians of Württemberg-Sigmaringen in the north and east would join up with the Baden people of the west and south. The result was the combined south-western state of Baden-Württemberg.
Nowadays the Black Forest has an ideal infrastructure for tourism, and is regarded as the perfect combination of a major cultural legacy, unspoiled natural beauty, and typical Baden-Württemberg hospitality, also reflected in the outstanding breadth and depth of the Württemberg and the Baden cuisine.

2. THE SOUTHERN BLACK FOREST

2.1 Freiburg, Schauinsland, Hofsgrund, Schniederlihof

Freiburg has earned itself many names
over the years, and this southern Baden city on the banks of the little River Dreisam has for a long time been thought of as the "Ecology Capital", and not only because of the numerous, environmentally-minded students who fill its streets. The excellent local passenger transport system of the RVF, the Regio Verkehrsbund Freiburg or regional integral transport system, offers tickets at low prices and has contributed its share to this reputation. Freiburg has also gained a reputation lately as a centre for research into and the use of solar energy.

Many travel guide-books enjoy describing Freiburg as the "metropolitan city of the Breisgau", or secret capital of the Black Forest, and this is attributable not only to its capacity as a crossroads for all means of transport. It is a major hub for the whole upper Rhine region, from Basle to Offenburg and for large parts of the southern Black Forest. It is still rightly entitled to call itself the **"Zähringen City",** just as one or two other towns in the region are. The typical "Zähringen cross-roads", the intersection of the two main streets in the city centre running from each of the four town gates, are an obvious testimony to this tradition.

The term "Sun City" is being used more and more often for this centre of the services sector on the upper Rhine. It might have been derived from the towns built in the American sun-belt with pensioners mainly in mind, and indeed there are many former students who, at the end of their working lives, find their way back there to the city with the highest quality of life they have known. This special quality of life, student enthusiasm aside, must be one of the reasons why the university city of Freiburg, along with Tübingen and Heidelberg, is at the top of the popularity scale.

Of course, these terse statements tell one far less about the character of a city than one can learn by visiting it. As soon as one arrives, one is struck by the "heavenly" position of the city, set as it is in the mild garden of the upper Rhine plain, with a climate sometimes comparable with that of the Mediterranean; the uplands of the Black Forest and even the Alps are just as close as the savoir-vivre and the fine cuisine of the French neighbours.

Freiburg nestles between the gentle hills and vineyards of the Kaiserstuhl to the west and the Black Forest sheltering it to the east. The nearest mountain, the Schauinsland (1,284 metres), is virtually in Freiburg's back yard.

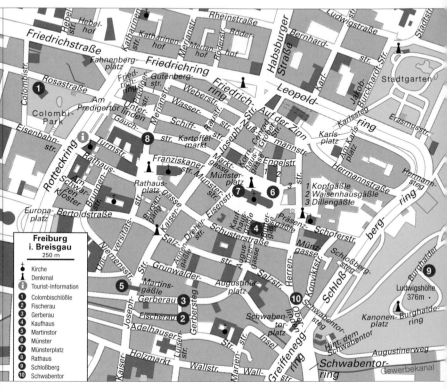

City Atlas of the Inner City of Freiburg

Despite its rich and turbulent history, the university city today presents a modern face. This is surely due to the students, who make up almost one-tenth of the total population, but there are still many buildings that bear testimony to the long and varied history of the city.

Freiburg Wirtschaft und Touristik GmbH

Rotteckring 14 · 79098 Freiburg
Tel. 07 61 / 3 88 18 80
Fax 07 61 / 3 70 03

HISTORY OF THE CITY OF FREIBURG

The city of Freiburg was founded in 1120 AD by Konrad II of Zähringen and his brother Bertold II. Like other Zähringen cities such as Offenburg and Villingen, it has the typical layout with two main streets connecting the town gates and intersecting at a right-angle in the middle. They still dominate the city centre today, and form a pedestrian precinct in the heart of the city.

Building work started in about 1200 on the **Minster,** which was later to be graced by "the most beautiful tower in Christendom", as the Basle art historian Jakob Burckhardt put it.

The last of the Zähringen dynasty, Bertold V, died childless in 1218, and this marks the start of the era of the "Counts of Freiburg", who were in turn succeeded by the Habsburgs in 1368. Plague raged through the town in the 14th century, and again in the 16th. At some time in the 14th century the Franciscan monk Bertold Schwarz is attributed with the invention of gunpowder, and a memorial to him now stands in the square in front of the town hall (Rathausplatz).

In 1457, Archduke Albrecht VI founded the university. Until the middle of the 16th century, the town was dominated by a number of major buildings which have been preserved down to the present day: the Kornhaus, the choir of the Minster, and the historic Kaufhaus (trading house) in the square next to the Minster (Münsterplatz). During the Thirty Years' War, Freiburg had only 2,000 inhabitants (in 1632), and by the time the war ended in 1648 it had been besieged and fought over five times. A Swedish army occupied it, and the French were later to rule over it, before finally (in 1698) it came into the hands of the Habsburgs.

Freiburg was not spared the fighting in the Baden Revolution of 1848, and shells and bombs fell on the city and took their toll in the first and second world wars. Other notable events in the less military side of the city's history were the completion of the railway station and the opening of the Offenburg-Freiburg railway in 1845. The first train ran through the rugged Höllental valley in 1887, and in 1930 the first cable-cabin heaved its way up to the top of the Schauinsland.

Freiburg was the capital of South Baden from 1946 to 1952, when a plebiscite in december 1951 determined that Baden should merge with Württemberg to form a single south-western State. The best way to gain an acquaintance with the city and its history is by walking around and through it. "Freiburg has what everyone is looking for" - this was the city's advertising slogan for many years, and in the summer one keeps being reminded of it because that is when so many people, and not just visitors from the surrounding region, wander happily around in "their" Freiburg. The city absolutely must appear on the programme of any tour of the Black Forest, and is also highly suitable as an intermediate stop for people going on holiday further south.

Freiburg has a charm of its own, whatever the season. It is at its most colourful and lively in high summer, when a Baden and international flair dominates its streets. Anyone who comes in the spring will find the spring is travelling to meet him in this mild climate. In the autumn, hikers and wine-lovers combine a visit to

INFORMATION

Opening times for the Freiburg Minster
Monday to Saturday, 10.00 am to 6.00 pm, Sunday 1.00 to 6.00 pm
Guided tours of the choir:
Monday to Friday at 11.00 and 2.30 pm

the city with excursions to the Kaiser-stuhl and the Black Forest. The wooded hills of course have plenty to offer in the winter as well, particularly for skiers - even weighed down with ski-boots, they can reach the ski-runs and cross-country skiing tracks quickly and easily with the tram and the Schauinsland cable-car.

The best place from which to start many activities in the city is **Münsterplatz,** which is also the start-point for our tour of the city. The building of the Minster stretched out over 300 years;

A view from the transept into the Choir with its striking net altar ➙

The Minster and the colourful hurly-burly of the market, seen from the west

it was one of the few churches in the upper Rhine on which building work started back in the Middle Ages (around 1200), and it was finally finished in 1513. The design at the start of the building work resembled a castle, in the late-Roman style and on the Basle model. By the time the work was completed - and it had even been interrupted for more than 100 years - it was dominated more by Gothic influences

The glass windows of the Minster contain pictures and coats-of-arms of the guilds. This is a reminder of the fact that the citizens themselves had become the masters of the town in the 13th century. A walk through the Minster must include time to admire the magnificent main door, richly decor-ated with sculptured figures. Medieval units of measure are also "eternalised" in it.

The windows in the nave were in many cases donated by guilds, as their presentation shows. On the inside of the west door one can see one of the Minster's finest gothic figures of the Madonna. The sculpture by F.X. Hauser depicting the Last Supper dates from 1795, and together with the high altar by Hans Baldung Grien represents the best-known treasures in the church interior.

No visitor should miss the opportunity of climbing the tower, 116 metres high, and gaining a magnificent view down over the colourful hurly-burly of the market and the neighbouring hills of the Black Forest, the Kaiserstuhl, and the Vosges.

We can start our city tour after descending the tower. On the north side of the square, where a market is held every day, it is

Opening times for the Minster tower
Sunday 1.00 to 5.00 pm, also:
April to September
Monday to Saturday, 9.30 am to 5.00 pm
October to March
Tuesday to Saturday, 10.00 am to 4.00 pm
but: closed Monday from October to March

traditionally the farmers from Freiburg, the surrounding Breisgau region, and the Kaiserstuhl who sell their regional produce. On the south side, stall-holders sell fruit (almost) regardless of the time of year. A striking feature of the Münsterplatz is the **Historical Trading House** (1520) on the south side. This is a late-gothic building plastered in red with brightly coloured bricks, and in the Middle Ages it was the focal point of business life; even today it serves as one of the most impressive buildings in the city for celebrations and special events.

Only a few yards away is the former home of the painter, sculptor, and architect J.C. Wentzinger, dating from 1761. Since 1994 it has housed the **Museum of Municipal History.**

**Opening times for the Museum of Municipal History
Tuesday to Sunday
10.00 am to 5.00 pm**

On the north side of the Münsterplatz one passes the city library and arrives at the Kornhaus, a corn barn with a striking stepped gable. It dates all the way back to 1498.

Any walk through the city must lead down **Kaiser Joseph Strasse,** nowadays the main shopping street and the heart of the pedestrian precinct, to the **Rathaus** (town hall). In the Rathausplatz, Bertold Schwarz, the well known monk and inventor of gunpowder, gazes down on the newly married couples who

The old and the new town halls form a well preserved historical group in the heart of the old centre of Freiburg

emerge almost every hour from the historic town hall. The Rathausplatz is flanked on the opposite side by the remains of the old Franciscan monastery, and is the place where jugglers and street musicians perform in the summer. Only a few yards behind the old and the new town hall one will find (if one looks carefully) the Gerichtslaube or courthouse, the oldest official building in the city, dating from 1303.

If one then crosses a busy main road, Rotteckring, into the **Colombipark,** one will come across the Colombi mansion, which since 1867 has housed the **Museum of prehistory and early history.**

The visitor can also walk along Rotteckring to the city's newly modernised theatre, past Bertold's fountain, and back to the central traffic axis, Kaiser Joseph Strasse, from where one can see another city landmark, the **Martinstor.** This is the older of the two surviving town gates, and nowadays form the gateway to one of the most idyllic corners of the old city centre of Freiburg.

The old houses in **Fischerau** and **Gerberau,** the two streets that branch off here along the old city walls, now contain small shops and cafés. Fischerau leads along the Gewerbekanal back to the second axis of the Zähringen cross-roads, and the Salzstrasse.

Little brooks and tiny alleyways make the town centre so attractive, and not only for children

Smart shops and cafés along the Fischerau, the old commercial canal, invite the visitor to stroll along by the water

There we find the **Augustine Museum** in a former Augustine monastery, exhibiting Upper Rhine art from the Middle Ages to the baroque period. And anyone who would like to make the leap back into the culture of our modern age will be at the right address in the **Museum of Modern Art** in the former Adelhauser school.

**Opening times for the Museum of
Prehistory and Early History
Augustine Museum
Museum of Modern Art
Tuesday to Sunday, 10.00 am to 5.00 pm**

This walk through Freiburg's history is rounded off with a stroll through the other historic town gate, the **Schwabentor,** at the foot of which the "Rote Bären" lays claim to the title of the oldest hostelry. It is only a few minutes on foot from here to the cannon emplacement of the **Schlossberg,** or castle hill, from where one has a magnificent view of the Minster and across the city, over the nearby Schönberg, and all the way to the Kaiserstuhl and the Vosges. And then it only takes a short time to return to the start-point of this tour, the Münsterplatz.

But what does this city have to offer those visitors who are not so keen on cultural monuments, and would like to meet people and see how the live? The range of possibilities is enormous. A tour of this kind starts best, once again, at the Münsterplatz, where one can overhear the Alemannic dialect and observe the southern Baden style of living.

Anyone who wants to see Alemannic high spirits at their best should go and watch the local football club, SC Freiburg, and see the local Freiburg "Bobbele" (dialect for "ordinary people") cheering them on for all they are worth. Alternatively, one can enjoy Freiburg people at their lustiest during the "fifth season" - the carnival season, known down here as "Fasnet". There is a long tradition of Fasnet clubs which organise processions through the streets and alleys of the city - one of the finest displays of Alemannic custom.

Further good occasions on which to visit Freiburg include the Freiburg Weinfest, on the first weekend in July, and the wine-tasting in the middle of August, when one can try a good cross-section of the Baden wine landscape. It is not only music enthusiasts that flood in by the thousand to the Tent Music Festival, from the end of June to the middle of July, but also more and more prominent performers. The concert house, near the mainline railway station, is developing visibly into an additional cultural centre of the city.

All the fun of the Volksfest can be enjoyed on the Messplatz when the spring or the autumn fair is in full swing; other places call this kind of event Jahrmarkt or Kirmes. And the Christmas market on the Rathausplatz is regarded as one of the finest in the whole of Germany.

Anyone who would like to see Freiburg from its quieter side will have plenty of opportunity to do so, well away from the city centre and all the festivities. The Eugen Keidel thermal baths just outside the city are one example; another is the planetarium on the roof of the technical college, or the quiet park landscape of Old Cemetery, laid out in 1683 in front of the town's defensive walls. The Black Forest stretches down into the outskirts of the city, and offers plenty of scope for anyone looking for an excursion out into Mother Nature. Two points of attraction lie practically on Freiburg's doorstep. The **Steinwasen Mountain Wildlife Park** lies in the Oberried valley, between Freiburg and Notschrei, and here one can observe local animals such as marmots and wild boar, or chamois and ibex leaping across the rocky slopes.

Travelling by cable-car up Freiburg's own private mountain, the Schauinsland, is an experience at any time of year

There is a special attraction for children - the 800-metre long summer toboggan-run. A chair-lift brings them and their toboggans to the top.

**Opening times for the
summer toboggan-run
May to September, 9.00 am to 6.00 pm
October to November, 10.00 am to 5.00 pm
December to April on request**

A special treat is waiting in the form of the city's "own private" mountain, the Schauinsland (1284 metres). It is shown in the Land Registry as part of the city of Freiburg, so that makes Freiburg the highest city in Germany. The name actually means "Look out across the countryside". The cable-railway to the top was opened in 1930 and completely modernised in 1988.
It is in the autumn in particular, when a thick blanket of fog often wraps the Rhine plain in monotonous grey for days on end, that

the ride to the sunlight summit is a stunning experience. The valley station in Günterstal can be reached by the buses and trams of the environmentally friendly RVF integrated transport network (as can all the sights listed in this tour), and from the valley to the station at the top of the **Schauinsland** only takes 20 minutes, so one is soon far from the madding crowds and can enjoy the clear Black Forest air in this popular hiking and skiing paradise.

Operating hours of the Schauinsland cable-cars

1st to 31st May: 9.00 am to 5.00 pm
1st June to 14th September: 9.00 am to 6.00 pm
15th September to 31st October: 9.00 am to 5.00 pm
1st November to 30th April: 9.30 am to 5.00 pm

But: not in operation in March, or from the middle of November to the middle of December.

Numerous mountain paths lead directly away from the top station, up to and around the summit, and back. In about 30 minutes one can reach the **Eugen Keidel tower,** named after a former Lord Mayor of the city. This modern wooden structure is topped by a viewing platform from which, on a clear day, one can see three of the highest peaks in the Swiss Alps: Eiger, Mönch, and Jungfrau.

Wind-battered beeches on the Schauinsland (1284 metres) - their bizarre shapes stand out particularly clearly in the winter

Even in summer, the **beech trees** on the Schauinsland remain bent over as a testimony to the raw wind that blows against these heights. In the winter the trees are covered by a suit of white armour, and look like pieces of surrealist art - to the delight of photographers.

The winter is of course the high season at the highest point of the city, and a cross-country skiing track called the Notschreiloipe is easily reached from the Schauinsland; one could say it is in Freiburg's back yard. People nowadays making a casual Sunday excursion to these heights can easily forget that this raw mountain region has not always been mainly at the service of amateur skiers and nature-lovers. The nearby hamlet of **Hofsgrund** used

Hofsgrund, part of Oberried, with its little pleasure lake, lies below the peak of the Schauinsland

to be mainly a mining community. This is because the Schauinsland mountains concealed lead ore and silver in their interior. The gangways are up to 700 years old; they have now been made easily accessible, and stretch out through the mountain to a total length of about 40 kilometres.

Mining was also the foundations of Freiburg's wealth in the Middle Ages, without which the Minster could never have been built. Part of the history of mining can be discovered in the **Schniederlihof,** an open-air and farming museum in a farmhouse built in 1592, shows how the farming family lived and worked in the highest farm in the Black Forest. It is only a short walk from here to the solar observatory on the Schauinsland, where guided tours are available in the summer.

The daily toil of the Black Forest miners is brought to life again by a visit to the Schniederlihof farmhouse and mining museum

Opening times for the Schniederlihof
10.00 am to 5.30 pm
May and June: Saturdays, Sundays, and public holidays. July and August: Every day
September: Tuesdays, Thursdays, Saturdays, Sundays, and public holidays.
October: Tuesdays, Saturdays, Sundays, and public holidays.

2. The southern Black Forest
2.2 Markgräflerland and Staufen

The **Markgräflerland** runs south of Freiburg all along the Swiss border almost as far as the Upper Rhine. It must be one of the most charming pre-Alpine zones on the Rhine valley side of the Black Forest. Because of its gently hilly character and mild climate, and because it is so dominated by wine-making, it is also called the "German Tuscany".

However, the region also has one or two other characteristics here that give it a touch of the Mediterranean: the influence of its neighbours to the south and the west - in cuisine, for instance. Or the hot springs in the spa towns along the edge of the Black Forest, offering relaxation and enjoyment. And, of course, the excellent wines, produced here in one of the southernmost wine-growing areas in Germany. They range from a simple, robust Gutedel to the fine, mature Spätburgunder.

The southern part of the badische Weinstrasse, the Wine Road linking so many Baden wine-growing towns, can be taken as a guide-line for exploring the Markgräflerland. It leaves Freiburg heading southwards, and leads first to **Bad Krozingen.** The use of the curative hot springs, here and in many other places, can be traced back to the days of Roman settlement.

Art-lovers are enraptured by the oldest wall-paintings in the Upper Rhine region, which can be seen in St Ulrich's chapel, part of the Glöcklehof in Oberkrozingen; this has been in the hands of various different monasteries over the centuries.

The mansion house in Unterkrozingen was built in 1579 and converted into the baroque style in the middle of the 18th century. It is now famous for its collection of historic keyboard instruments.

Historic keyboard instruments have been collected for exhibition in the mansion of Unterkrozingen

One of the most beautiful places from which to explore the Markgräflerland is the little town of **Staufen,** traditionally associated with the Faust legend. It nestles in a sheltered position at the entrance to the Münster valley, one of the finest gateways to the Black Forest; it leads up at its further end to the Belchen, a mountain 1,414 metres high with one of the most extensive views anywhere in the region. Staufen sits at the foot of vineyard-

The ruined Staufenburg crowns the vineyards growing up the Schlossberg

covered hills, the most striking one being the Schlossberg, covered in vines and featuring the ruins of the old castle, and has preserved its historic town centre to this day. Cars are not allowed into the central area, and the pedestrian precinct invites the visitor to stroll past (and to enter) its large number of small and original shops. Legend has it that it was here that Faust made his pact with the devil in 1529 - to be precise, in Room 5 of the local pub, the Gasthaus zum Löwen in the main street. A plaque on the façade makes a reference to this saga.

The pedestrian precinct of the little town, made famous by the Faust legend, invites the visitor to take a quiet stroll

In the market place, one can find the Stubenhaus, now the town's museum displaying its history since Celtic days.

Other places also worth seeing are a small museum of ceramics and the Staufenburg castle ruins, reached with a short walk (45 minutes there and back) from the town centre. One can also strengthen oneself here ready for longer excursions: the "Wiiwegli" (Alemannic dialect for "Weinweg", the Wine Road, stretches another 53 kilometres from here over the vine-covered hills with the finest views and all the way to Weil am Rhein. Travelling through these hills, one soon reaches the little town of Grunern and then the mining town of Sulzburg, where the former Evangelical town church (built in 1834) now houses the Baden-Württemberg State Mining Museum. The visitor can follow the whole course of the region's salt and ore mining history here.

Opening times for the Stubenhaus museum
Monday to Friday, 9.00 am to 12.00
noon and 2.00 to 5.00 pm
Saturdays and Sundays, 3.00 to 6.00 pm

Mining museum
Every day except Monday, 2.00 to 5.00 pm

This little town became famous through the church of St Cyriak, a witness of the Otto epoch. From 1008 onwards it served as the church of the Benedictine monastery, and became the Evangelical parish church in 1550.

Above the town, near a camp-site, an old Jewish cemetery dating from 1550 reminds us that Sulz-burg used to be the home of many Jewish citizens, although they were not allowed to live in Freiburg, for instance. The synagogue has been preserved, although badly damaged but now restored. It stands in the Mühlbachstrasse, and is available for cultural events.

Another important stopping-point on the way further south is **Heitersheim,** once the residence of Knights of St John of Malta, although one has to leave the terrace road through the vineyards and all its fine views to descend into the plain of the Upper Rhine. The Knights resided here for a long time, and part of the castle dating from the 16th century is still preserved. The gatehouse and keep of the moated medieval castle can still be discerned clearly, and the baroque chancellery building on the south side is regarded as the display piece of this little wine-making town.

Müllheim, the next stopping-point on our journey through the southern Markgräflerland, is nowadays a modern centre for service industries but has still retained its charm as a wine-making centre. Its two faces are reflected in the annual Müllheim Sekt market, when the region's finest sparkling produce is presented. The typical vinestock of the region is the Gutedel, and of course it has to appear here in the form of a Sekt.

The Marktgräfer museum of wine and local arts and crafts is well worth seeing, with exhibits documenting the history of wine-making in the everyday lives of southern Baden people.

Opening times for the Marktgräfer Museum, Mühlheim of Wine and Local Arts and Crafts April to October, Tuesday 3.00 to 6.00 pm All year round on Sunday 3.00 to 6.00 pm

It is an unforgettable experience to enjoy the Markgräflerland countryside from the air, and Fritz Klank can enable you to float silently above it in a balloon. This balloon pilot lives in Müllheim

gers out over the vineyards and the meadows wherever the wind dict-ates. Flights also start occasionally from the Upper Black Forest, and he will be glad to "give you a lift".

The remains of the Roman way of bathing have been well preserved in **Baden-weiler,** and can be inspected in the park directly alongside the modern thermal baths. The castle ruins, likewise in the park, offer a fine view of the town, the Rhine plain, and the Vosges.

It is easy to travel from here to one of the most outstanding viewing points in the southern Black Forest, and the castle of Bürgeln, 10 kilometres further south, offers a very fine view indeed.

A view inside the castle will reveal a magnificent interior with fine stucco decorations.

Opening times for Schloss Bürgeln
Guided tours from
18th. of November Penitence and Prayer Day
11.00 am, 2.00, 3.00, 4.00, and 5.00 pm
Closed on Tuesdays

In **Schliengen,** only a few more kilometrés southwards and set on one of the sunny terraces of the Markgräflerland, wine is the tre of focus. In an English-style park there stands the moated grange of Entenstein, dating from 1407 and serving today as the local town hall. **Bad Bellingen's** history as a spa town does not

stretch all that far back; the hot springs were not discovered until 1955, and then only when the drillers were looking for oil. On the other hand, this town is the home of the Upper Rhine Spa Museum, where one can follow the history of spas in the Black Forest, the Vosges, and the Swiss Jura from Roman days onwards. This southern route reaches its

Opening times for the Oberrheinisches Bäder- und Heimatmuseum, Bad Bellingen/Bamlach Wednesday and Sunday, 2.00 to 5.00 pm and on request

delightful end in a **triangle** of **Efringen-Kirchen, Kandern,** and **Blansingen,** where everything is once again to be found that makes the Markgräflerland so enchanting. Efringen-Kirchen was praised long ago by the local southern Baden poet Johann Peter Hebel as a paradise-garden. The high place held by wine-making here is documented by the Markgräflerland District Cellars, where almost 10 million litres of local wine are marketed. An excurs-ion to the pottery town of Kandern leads us back to the edge of the Black Forest, where we can visit the museum of ceramics and local arts and crafts and try the bakers' speciality, Kandner Bretzel. The "Chanderli" is a historic steam-drawn rail-way train that runs several times a year between Weil and Kan-

Opening times for the Heimat und Keramikmuseum, Kandern April to October, Wednesday 3.00 to 5.30 pm, Sunday 10.00 to 12.30 am Guided tours on request. Tel 07626/89960

dern. In Blansingen, finally, we encounter the traces of ancient culture in the Upper Rhine with the wall paintings in the tiny, single-nave village church, which dates from the 15th century.

2. The southern Black Forest
2.3: Münstertal, Belchen,
Wiesental, Todtnau, Feldberg

One of the most beautiful ways into the mountains of the Black Forest leads through a long, winding valley, the **Münstertal.** As soon as one leaves Staufen and heads up the valley one can see the round dome of the Belchen, which here once again places a crown on the silhouette of the Black Forest.

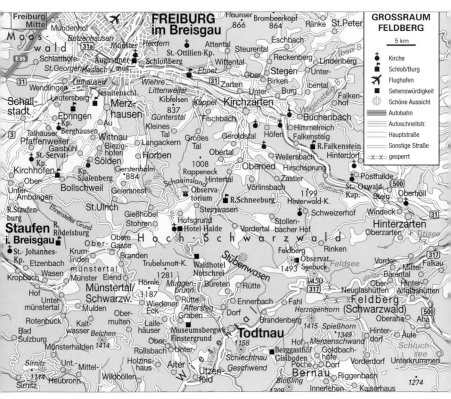

Atlas of Feldberg and Surrounding Area

Not long after leaving the picturesque town of Staufen, famous from the Faust legend, one is already in the deepest parts of the Black Forest. Both the valley and the eponymous village owe their name to the Benedictine monastery of St Trudpert, founded as long ago as 640 AD and situated between the villages of Untermünstertal and Obermünstertal.

The little community went through something of a golden age in the 12th century. Silver ore was mined in the area, to the envy of the Freiburg citizens, who thought their wealth might be in jeopardy. In the 14th century the Freiburg people found a quick and effective way of dealing with the troublesome competition in mining, minting coins, and trading in silver: they attacked the town and burnt it to the ground. However, the town, the mine, and the monastery survived and flourished again for a while, until the declining significance of silver mining robbed Münstertal of its status as a town, and it reverted to that of a village. Nevertheless, Münstertal has now regained importance as a tourist centre with numerous sights worth seeing and two unusual museums: bee-keeping, and a silver mine open to visitors.

In the 13th century, the town was the place where 500 to 1,000 miners lived and worked. Silver mining in the shafts dating back to the 11th century virtually came to an end with the discovery of America, although up to 400 miners were still employed when the mine finally closed its doors in the 1960s. It is now once again possible to see the "Schindlergang", one of the main working levels of the Teufelsgrund mine, and first mentioned in 1512. The machinery and tools give a vivid impression of the way the work was done down the mines.

Opening times for the Teufelsgrund mine

15th June to 15th September:
every day except Monday, 2.00 to 5.00 pm
1st April to 14th June and 16th September to 31st October:
Tuesday, Thursday, Saturday, and Sunday, 2.00 to 5.00 pm.

The "healthy" air in the mine galleries is still put to good use nowadays; asthma patients spend about an hour and a half in one called the Friedrichstollen every day, on account of the damp, germ-free air. Those who prefer the outdoor version of Nature, however, can explore a path 17 kilometres long, through geological and mining history, along the valley and find many pointers to the history of mining that for so long dominated the valley and the town.

In the midst of the green landscape between Untermünstertal and Obermünstertal is the "monasterium" of St Trudpert, the majestic architecture of which rises majestically above the farms in the valley. Its foundation, early in the 7th century, can be traced back to a monkish settlement at the grave of the Irish missionary Trudpert. Expanded and renovated many times over, the monastery was finally destroyed in the Thirty Years' War, except for the Choir (1465).

Then in the 18th century it was rebuilt by the architect Peter Thumb. The new nave of the church is the prime example of his work, but the striking onion dome of the tower dates from his time as well. The pulpit of the Benedictine abbey originally came from St Augustine's church in Freiburg. The body of the church has no transept, and is fairly plain, with discreet stucco work.

Colourful frescoes narrate the life of St Trudpert, and the early-classical stucco and marble High Altar is of significance to art historians. The abbey is now the parent house of the nuns of St. Josef.

Another sight worth seeing in Münstertal is the museum of bee-keeping, in the former Obermünstertal town hall. This collection is regarded as being unique in Europe; covering more than 200 square metres, it not only documents the life and work of this industrious insect but also allows visitors to observe them in their hives.

The town hall in Untermünstertal houses a museum of forestry, with a scale model of a charcoal kiln as is often built even nowadays in one of the side valleys.

 **Opening times for the Museum of Bee-Keeping All year round, Wednesday, Saturday, Sunday, and public holidays 2.00 to 5.00 pm Museum of Forestry June to October, Wednesday and Saturday, 2.00 to 5.00 pm November to May by prior agreement**

From Münstertal the road twists steeply upwards, each hairpin providing a new and magnificent view, to one of the highest and most beautiful viewing-points in the Black Forest, the **Belchen** (1,414 metres). The road up to the summit is closed at weekends, so the visitor must climb either into a shuttle bus or on his or her own two feet to the top.

The climb is rewarded with a magnificent view out across the Rhine valley to the Vosges. On autumn days, if the air at ground level is colder than at this level, thick clumps of fog cover the plain but the view across them is often specially good. To the south one can see the snow-covered chain of Alpine peaks all the way from the Säntis in northern Switzerland to Mont Blanc, on the French side of the Alps.

On clear days one can see right across to the Alps from the top of the Belchen

However, even if the weather does not permit quite such a magnificent view, the climb to the top of this mountain is an experience in itself. The characteristic round top, the counterpart to the suitably named "balloons" on the Alsace side, looks down on the west side of the Black Forest over the Wiesental and the Münstertal, as well as many others.

For many hikers and winter-sports enthusiasts, the Belchen is the most demanding but also the most beautiful stage in their tour. Beneath its heights, the Westweg runs from Basle up to Pforzheim, and in February every year the most insatiable of them all appear here on their "rucksack race": carrying a weight of 5 kilos in their rucksacks, they cover the distance of 100 kilometres from Schonach to the Belchen and back.

The **Wiesental,** which starts at the foot of the Belchen, offers an enchanting combination of all the types of landscape between the Upper Black Forest and the Upper Rhine. **Schönau** is the start-point in a line of valleys where one can, incidentally, follow a well marked hiking route called the Wiesentalweg.

The signs, with a green triangle on a white background, lead one from Schopfheim all the way up to the Feldberg. Anyone who turns off down into a valley between any two villages can easily return by public transport to the start-point, and can make a beautiful hiking tour of the Black Forest without too much exertion.

Schönau is also very suitable as a base from which to explore the Upper Black Forest. The historic town centre with its stylish town hall and the "Wiesental Minster" are in invitation to look round. The church dates from the first years of this century, but retains the early gothic style. It was originally established by the monastery in St Blasien. The High Altar is well worth seeing; it dates from 1530, and parts of a late Gothic Altar of St Mary are integrated into it.

A diversion to Zell and **Schopfheim,** the former town of the Markgrafs, leads all the way down almost to the Rhine itself. In the old centre of this modern industrial town one can still find numerous houses dating from the 16th century, and even the remains of the former castle have been preserved. The Kornhaus, near the church, has been carefully restored and is now a school. Up the valley from Schopfheim is the village of **Hausen.** The southern Baden people, being the direct descendants of Alemannic tribes, link this name with a great deal of history and poetry. As the home village of the prelate and poet Johann Peter Hebel it now possesses the house in which he was born, now a memorial to his name, and the museum of local arts and crafts in a half-timbered house on the corner of Hebelstrasse and Bahnhofstrasse.

The birthplace of the poet Johann Peter Hebel in Hausen

Opening times of the Hebel Memorial and Museum of Local Arts and Crafts

Sunday, 10.00 to 12.00 noon
Monday to Saturday by prior agreement.

Further up the valley is Todtnau, the birthplace of German ski-ing. The first German ski club was founded here in 1891, and still to this day it is the venue of the FIS World Cup race. It can be sure of plenty of snow, and with its numerous lifts and well tended ski-runs it is a real Mecca for Alpine ski-ers in particular.

However, it was a man from the Westphalian plains, of all people, who set the development of the sport of ski-ing in motionmamore than a hundred years ago. Mr Tholus, once a ship's doctor, had settled here and, making his arduous way through deep snow to outlying farmhouses, remembered reading during his travels about wooden planks called "skier" being in wide use in northern Europe. In 1888 the Norwegian polar explorer Fridtjof Nansen crossed Greenland on skis, and soon the whole world was talking about these ingenious wooden planks. The next steps were taken very quickly: the first ski club was founded, and Nansen was even its first honorary member. Today there are 40 kilometres of carefully trended pistes (ski-runs), 22 ski lifts, and about 60 kilometres of Loipen (cross-country ski-ing routes), not to mention 80 kilometres of paths sufficiently cleared of snow to allow winter hiking.

There is a special attraction to be found in Aftersteg, a village attached to Todtnau, on the road that leads to the Schauinsland. Here one can enter a glass foundry and watch how glowing lumps of molten glass are blown into artistic, filigree shapes. From there, and from the village of Todtnauberg, one can also reach the waterfall, which is almost 100 metres high. From Todtnau a chair-lift leads up to the nearest mountain, the Hasenhorn, the start-point for some beautiful hiking tours.

The water of the Todtnau waterfalls crashes down nearly 100 metres

The only place that can out-rank Todtnau as a winter sports centre is **Feldberg.** The slopes of this mountain, at 1,494 metres the highest in the Black Forest, are integrated into the ski-ing circus of Todtnau. "The Highest", as it is respectfully known, has plenty to offer outside the winter months as well. It sits like a spider at the centre of a widespread network of hiking paths, carefully tended by the members of the Black Forest Association, and criss-crossing long-distance hiking paths and Loipen here in the largest nature-protection area in the Black Forest. The Feldberg Road, the shortest holiday road in Baden-Württemberg with only about 15 kilometres to its name, running from Titisee to Feldberg, but it covers an area of more than 3,000 hectares that has been under a protection order since 1937. The Feldberg is not hard to climb. It is only a few hundred metres from the car-park to a chair-lift with which one can swing up to the **Bismarck tower** near the top. There is a steep climb downwards to the **Feldsee,** formed in Ice Age on the north wall of the Feldberg, and to an area of marsh alongside it.

Hiking and walking around the top of the Feldberg is less of a strain. The rich soils within the sub-Alpine "dry island" offer a habitat to numerous animals and plants which would not otherwise find a home in our latitudes.

The pink Troddelblume is one of these relics from the Ice Age, but its smaller relation, the blue Zwergtroddelblume is an "immigrant" from the Alpine region.

More than a thousand chamois live in the region around the peak, where a rougher climate prevails than in other parts of the Black Forest. Gales can gust up to 150 k.p.h. or more, and in many years the last traces of the snow will still be in sight well into May.

The Bismarck Tower represents the highest point of the Feldberg (1494 metres)

A relict of the Ice Age - the Feldsee at the foot of the Feldberg

The round peak is not bare, as one might expect, because trees have no chance against the wind and weather. In fact, human beings are once again the cause, having used even the highest levels for decades as pasture for animals.

Because more and more people come to visit "The Highest" in particular, precautions started to be taken here at an early stage to protect Nature. The Feldberg Ranger, a graduate in forestry studies, introduces groups of visitors to the idiosyncrasies of this vulnerable area. He keeps a sharp eye open to ensure that the visitors keep to the rules - and, in particular, to the signposted paths.

And, because there is hardly anywhere else in Baden-Württemberg where one is closer to the heavens, the Feldberg is also the place where Germany's highest-place church is to be found. The "Church of the Transfiguration of Christ" was built in 1963, with a spire reminiscent of a Black Forest pine tree.

2. The southern Black Forest
2.4 Todtmoos, St. Blasien, Bernau, Präg, Grafenhausen, Wutach, Schluchsee, Altglashütten, Lenzkirch

South of the Feldberg, the landscape takes on the character most often associated with the name of the Upper Black Forest: mountain tops offering fine views, an alternation between wooded and open slopes that is a delight to the eye, and fine old farmhouses dominate the scene.

Todtnau is a suitable starting-point for a tour all round the Feldberg on its sunny side. Only a few kilometres down the valley from Wiesental brings one to Geschwend. No guide-book and no map will list any great sights to see here, but there is hardly corner of the Black Forest that offers so many old original 18th-century Black Forest farmhouses so well preserved.

A narrow, twisting little road leads to the little village of Präg. At the end of the last Ice Age, more than 10,000 years ago, six glacier-rivers ran together here from the peaks of the Black Forest, leaving behind the **Präg** basin, a typical Black Forest sight, and not only on account of its magnificent landscape.

The enormous masses of ice fashioned the hard granite into gentle hills. Valleys were scoured out where the streams of ice flowed together, the melting waters left behind impressive scree slopes, and the little lakes turned into flat marshes and wetlands. The mountain pastures around the little village provide the habitat for a large number of rare animal and plant species that otherwise only occur at high altitudes.

A short but informative walk takes one from the middle of the village, with its imposing old Black Forest houses, on a circular tour all round the Präg basin in about an hour.

Treasures of a totally different kind can be found in **Bernau,** reached in only a few minutes along a picturesque little road. Hans Thoma (1839 to 1924), probably the best-known painter from the Black Forest, started his life here as a farmer's son and went on to become a university professor, the director of an art gallery, and Privy Councillor to the Archdukes of Baden.

A museum is dedicated to him in the village of Innerlehen which documents the artist's life and work. Pictures full of the atmosphere of the Black Forest are in some cases from the hands of Hans Thoma Prize-winners or artists of a similar genre. The house in which Thoma was born can be found in Oberlehen, and one can still see many places in this district that appear in his paintings.

Opening times for the Hans Thoma Museum

Tuesday to Friday, 10.00 am to 12.00 noon and 2.00 to 5.00 pm
Saturday, Sunday, and public holidays, 10.30 am to 12.00 noon and 2.00 to 5.00 pm.

In Oberlehen one can also see the Reesenhof museum of local arts and crafts, housed in an 18th-century farmhouse that was inhabited until 1976 and is still in almost its original farmhouse condition. The museum displays not only the everyday lives of the people who lived and worked here but also a cross-section of the craftsmanship of farming people in the region: a cobbler's workshop, and tools for making brushes, barrels, or wooden roof-tiles.

Opening times for the Reesenhof Museum of Local Arts and Crafts

1st May to 30th June, and 1st September to 31st October, Tuesday to Sunday, 2.00 to 5.00 pm 1st July to 31st August, Tuesday to Saturday, 10.00 am to 12.00 noon and 2.00 to 5.00 pm; Sunday 2.00 to 5.00 pm 1st November to 30th April, Wednesdays and Sundays, 2.00 to 4.00 pm

Todtmoos, a health-holiday town with a bracing climate only a few kilometres further south, has developed into a meeting-place for dog-sled racers from all over the world.

On the last weekend in January, teams of huskies race along the snow-covered course and attract a larger crowd every year. Winter is the busy season in this town at the foot of the Hochkopf (1263 metres).

Todtmoos has a long tradition behind it as a spa and holiday resort

At any time of year, however, the baroque pilgrimage church of Our Dear Lady draws visitors into a sheltered valley, the Wehratal. It dates from the 13th century, and has been through many changes, the last of which was a thorough reconstruction in baroque times.

Todtmoos has a long tradition as a centre for health-holidays. The first spa hotels were opened here in 1863, and nowadays it is not only the healthy climate that draws the visitors; in addition to the museum of local arts and crafts and the historic vicarage there is also an observatory to visit (guided tours on request). 300-year-old Schwarzwald farmhouses wait to welcome visitors as well, who can also walk through romantic narrow gorges with waterfalls in the immediate vicinity, such as the Wehratalschlucht, between Todtmoos-Au and Wehr, which is one of the most impressive mountain valleys anywhere in Germany.

Magnificent displays of flowers decorate the old farmhouses

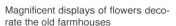

The valleys of the Wehra to the west and the Schwarza to the east mark the borders of the southern region of the Upper Black Forest, called the Hotzenwald. It is famous for its deeply incised valleys, and breath-taking view right out across the Alps, and its unique human history. The aboriginal Alemannic tribes that lived here, and still do, are regarded as obstinate, kind, and reliable. Their love of freedom and their obstreperousness have a long history. The Salpeter rebels rose up in the 18th century against the rule of the **monastery of St Blasien.**

St Blasien, with its huge hemispherical dome, is still today the main centre of the Hotzenwald. This is the third-largest domed church in the whole of Europe, and endows the village between the slopes of the Black Forest with a character all its own. There were settlers here as long ago as the 8th century, and in 858 AD the Benedictine monastery was given the relics of St Blasius, from whom the village takes its name.

The monastery was rebuilt from 1727 to 1747 in a rectangular shape. The monastery church was given its present-day appearance after a fire in 1768, when the bulky classical central part was built. The most impressive view of the dome can be gained from the interior of the circular church, which has a diameter of 36 metres. Borne by 20 Corinthian columns, the interior is flooded with light an contrasts delightfully with the intimacy of the Choir. Concerts are held here regularly in the summer.

Just as the cathedral-like Benedictine abbey of St Blasien reflects the history of the Black Forest, so also one will find a picture of ordinary rural life not far away in **Grafenhausen.** The attraction here is the **"Hüsli"**, a picture-book farmhouse that was already of interest to Black Forest visitors long before it featured in the successful television series "Black Forest Clinic".

← The dome of St Blasien is gigantic, and flooded with light. The dome is one of the largest of its kind anywhere

The "Hüsli" museum of local arts and crafts near Grafenhausen was famous long before it was used for making the television series "Black Forest Hospital"

The **Museum of Local Arts and Crafts** is accommodated in a Black Forest house which contains authentic ceiling paintings, original wall-cupboards, wainscoting, tiled stoves, and samples of folk-art. However, it was not built by some prosperous farmer centuries ago but in 1912, for an opera singer from Berlin. The exhibits were brought together lovingly and with great historical know-ledge, and the complete home, in which the great lady lived herself from 1945 to 1966, is now an impressive collection and well worth seeing.

Milling museum with farmhouse garden at the Tannenmühle

The "Hüsli" museum of local arts and crafts near Grafenhausen was famous long before it was used for making the

INFORMATION

Opening times for the Grafenhausen Museum of Local Arts and Crafts

1st October to 31st March
Tuesday to Saturday, 10.00 am to 12.00 noon and 1.30 to 5.00 pm Sundays and public holidays, 1.30 to 5.00 pm 1st April to 30th September, Tuesday to Saturday, 9.30 am to 12.00 noon and 1.30 to 5.30 p.m, Sundays and public holidays, 1.30 to 5.30 pm.

In the foothills of the Hotzenwald, the Black Forest is quieter and gentler. Further to the east, at **Bonndorf,** is where the Baar starts; this is a plateau between the Black Forest and the Swabian Alb, where the high chains of mountains are replaced by a gently rolling plateau where everything seems to be quieter and calmer.

It is therefore all the more of a surprise to come across a deep incision further to the east, the valley where the **Wutach** river has carved out a gorge. This is a dramatic landscape, with steep limestone cliffs up to 50 metres high. The footpath crosses the river seven times, and at a number of points along the bank it has to be secured with railings and wire cables.

The damp, greenhouse-like atmosphere enables the undergrowth to flourish like a jungle. Rare plants such as hart's-tongue, rock carnation, gentian, or Turk's-truss find their homes here, and the various different sub-climates along the gorge explain the fact that plants can be found here from every part of world, from the Arctic circle to the Mediterranean; botanists have identified about 1,200 different species.

Having been left in its natural state, the gorge is an oasis for many threatened species. 500 different species of butterfly have been counted, and rare birds such as migratory hawks and Arctic birds are just as much at home here as chamois. Parts of the gorge have been under nature conservancy orders since 1939.

One of the most beautiful entrances to the **Wutach gorge** is atSchattenmühle, near the Lotenbachklamm. From Bonndorf one travels through Boll directly into the valley, where it almost seems too deep for the little Wutach river. This river rises at an altitude of 1,450 metres, high up on the Feldberg, runs as a little brook into the Titisee lake, leaves it under the name of Gutach, and only becomes the Wutach where it empties into the Haslach. It owes its dramatic appearance to the glaciers that withdrew from the region about 10,000 years ago and sent huge quantities of melt-water into the valleys.

Another point of entry into the Wutach gorge is on the road just beyond **Lenzkirch.** The nearby Ursee valley offers an excursion to the Ursee lake, which borders on one of the few marshes that have been left behind as a relic of the Ice Age. A fine view can be gained from the Stossfelsen, a cliff-top that can be reached in 20 minutes from the nearby Raitenbuch.

Bird's-eye view of Lenzkirch - the little town at the foot of the Hochfirst includes the nature conservancy area of Urseemoor

Pure, idyllic Black Forest can also be enjoyed on the banks of a small lake, the Windgfällweiher, which can be reached on the way from **Raitenbuch** to **Altglashütten.** Hidden deep in the forest, this is another remnant of the Ice Age with its own special flora and fauna. Being only 64 acres in size, it is the smallest and calmest of the lakes in the triangle it forms with Titisee and Schluchsee. It is easy to walk round it or row across it.

The visitor can now travel via Altglashütten, which with its ski-lifts and Loipen has developed into a centre for winter sports, and then turn along the bank of the **Schluchsee** and thus to the foot of the Feldberg. The small town of Schluchsee not only has direct access to the lake, a bathing beach, and water sports facilities, but also an excellent range of hiking and winter sports facilities.

This includes well marked hiking paths all round the lake and, for instance, horse-sledge rides, a toboggan run, a natural skating rink, and Loipen. From the bathing beach one can explore the lake on board a small passenger boat, or hire a small boat and do one's own rowing. Water-lovers big and small owe this pleasure to a dam that has made the Schluchsee, with about 1,5 square miles of water, the largest lake in the Black Forest.

A centre not only for water-sports and skiing - the Schluchsee

2. Southern Black Forest
2.5 Titisee, Hinterzarten, Höllental, Hirschsprung, Hofgut Sternen

Titisee, the Feldberg, and Schluchsee - for the visitor to the Black Forest they form a magic triangle in the mountains above Freiburg, from where they can be reached quickly and easily by car or rail and enjoy picture-book views of the Black Forest.

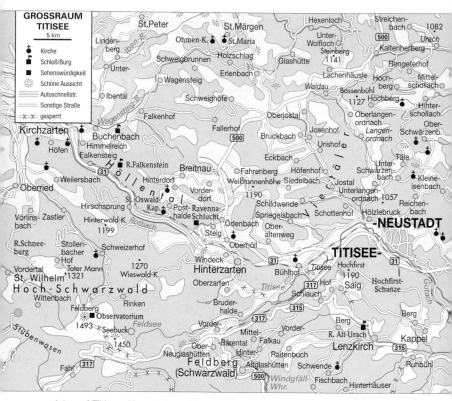

Atlas of Titisee-Neustadt and Surrounding Area

For a long time, the **Höllental** was the eye of the needle, the only valley leading east-west through the Black Forest. But today's traveller does not need to worry; it has long lost its terrors, and it is easy to climb this steep but direct route into the Upper Black Forest.

It has not always been easy. The Black Forest was an uninhabited area for thousands of years. Even the Romans seem to have been wary of the silva nigra, and the Alemannic tribes that settled around the foothills had no links with the settlements up on the Baar.

It was not until the Zähringen dukes came into the Breisgau that they maintained contacts via the Eschbachtal and the Glottertal to their home land of Swabia.

Trains and cars wind their twisting ways through the Höllental

Monks and farmers started taking over the forest about 1,000 years after the Romans. The Höllental was not opened up until the Middle Ages. There had been a cart track through it in 1638, but it was the daughter of the Austrian Empress, Marie Antoinette, who opened the portal of the Höllental in the 18th century. In order for her to travel from Vienna to Paris, a road had to be prepared suitable for a horse-drawn carriage, and the cart track became a metalled road.

Perhaps it was in those days that the descriptive place-names came into being that one can read along this route. Just after Kirchzarten there is a railway station called Himmelreich ("Heaven"), and after the ruined castle of Falkensteig there is **Hirschsprung ("Stag's Leap")** where a bronze stag stands guard on the steep cliff wall. There one is truly in "Heaven" - if the name of the place is anything to go by. The traveller's gaze is drawn as if by magic to the magnificent stag gazing down from the "Stag's Leap" on the busy traffic below. He is supposed once to have escaped from a huntsman by making this daring leap over the steep abyss.

Nowadays this eye of a needle represents no danger to the railway, road, and young Dreisam river passing through it.

Driving up the dramatic sections of this almost Alpine road, one cannot but feel respect for the engineers that built it. The railway line runs through numerous tunnels and across artistic bridges such as the **Ravenna viaduct.** The view alone makes the rail journey interesting, and when travelling from Freiburg towards Hinterzarten one should definitely try to obtain a window seat on the right-hand side.

Work started on building the **Höllental railway** in 1884, for which the railway engineer Robert Gerwig put his great experience on building the Gotthard railway to good use, and in 1887 Friedrich I, Archduke of Baden, inaugurated the stretch

The bronze stag stands guard over the narrows part of the

from Freiburg to Neustadt. Special locomotives operated both conventionally and in rack-and-pinion mode in order to tackle the enormous gradient. Because the route was so impressive, two panorama carriages were provided. It was not until 1933 that it became technically possible to do without the rack-and-pinion system.

A number of tunnels were needed. Shortly before the end of the valley, the railway crosses the **Ravenna gorge,** through which a waterfall roars down into the Höllental. The viaduct, with its six slender arches, is still regarded as a technical masterpiece as well as being one of the most beautiful of all railway structures. After crossing it, the railway still has to go through several tunnels and bends before reaching Hinterzarten, at an altitude of 900 metres.

Even today, a train journey along this stretch is still an experience, particularly since double-decker carriages came into use on it. The road is wide and almost straight for a considerable distance, but then has to cope with the steep climb with many narrow hairpin bends.

One such climb can be found at the entrance to the Ravenna gorge, where one can also find a historic building called the Hofgut Sternen - once a lonely farmhouse, now housing a modern restaurant and a glass-blowing works.

This craft has a long tradition in the Black Forest, where all the necessary raw materials were on hand: quartz sand from the brooks, beechwood which could be burnt to provide potash for mixing and melting with the quartz sand, and pine and spruce wood for the melter's fire.

Today, in the Hofgut Sternen, one can watch fine glassware being produced, to the customer's special request if necessary. The Hinterzarten Path is informative and well signposted, and also gives access to the Ravenna Gorge.

Filigree works of art are conjured up by the glass-blowers in the Sternenhof

The name of this wild gorge, so redolent of the age of romanticism and with such an Alpine character, does not come from Italy but is derived from "Rabenbach" - "Ravens' Brook". The innkeper of the Hofgut Sternen, Adolf Faller, started laboriously opening up the Ravenna gorge in 1875, and in 1920 the Black Forest Association made the path safe with steps and railings.

From the Ravenna gorge to **Hinterzarten** and beyond, one can enjoy the most impressive part of the Höllental route whether one is travelling on foot (on the Hinterzarten Path), by rail, or in a car. When one arrives in Hinterzarten one is in the middle of the Upper Black Forest, as one can tell even without reading the imposing collection of hiking-path signposts outside the station.

The little town itself combines the glamour of an old spa town, such as one can still find in the Parkhotel Adler, with the flair of a modern winter sport centre. High above it towers a ski-jump, the Adlerschanze, where international competitions are held every year. The Loipen all around the home town of two Olympic prize-winners and world champions, Georg Thoma and the younger Dieter Thoma, offer long excursions across the plateau. Hinterzarten is the venue of the Black Forest Ski Marathon and the 100-kilometre Rucksack Walk. Spectacular sledding races are held at the foot of the ski-jump.

There has been a **Skiing Museum** here since 1997, recording the history of the "white sport".

Opening times of the Hinterzarten Skiing Museum
Wednesday and Friday 3.00 to 6.00 pm
Saturday and Sunday and public holidays 12.00 noon to 6.00 pm.

The town has been highly popular recently with a different group of amateur sports fans. Mountain biking has been growing in popularity, and here there is a wide range of facilities on offer from bike hire and special training courses to highly detailed maps showing the recommended routes. Even the winter sports champion Georg Thoma, who incidentally made a loving film recently about his home town to celebrate his 60th birthday, offers facilities for mountain bikers.

Less spectacular, but no less interesting, is the Hinterzarten Hochmoor, an area of marsh within walking distance from the town centre or a few minutes from the railway station. It is home to many rare species of dragonfly and plants that have "immi-grated" from other regions. The path round the marsh is well signposted, and presents a piece of unspoilt Nature where time seems to have stood still. The area from Hinterzarten to the Feldberg also offers many longer hiking tours, lasting a half-day or a full day.

Titisee in the summer offers bathers delights to rival the Mediterranean: a bathing beach, boats for hire, and excursions, everything that makes such a stretch of water an attractive destination. There is also the fantastic back-drop of the Black Forest's highest mountain, and a picturesque little town that has virtually banned motor traffic for the benefit of its guests.

One big plus-point in Titisee's favour, which has now grown together with the neighbouring town of **Neustadt,** is that it is very readily accessible by car or rail, only a short distance from Freiburg.

One can explore the Titisee with a pedalo or on board a steamer

Titisee is about 2,5   kilometres long and 250 metres wide, making it the biggest natural lake in the German mountains. Trips on excursion boats start from the beach promenade in the middle of the town and last about half an hour.

Rowing and electric-powered boats are also on hire. Anyone who fancies the walk all round the lake needs to allow about an hour and a half; the path is well signposted.

The true heart of this spa town lies on the bank of the lake. Where once motor traffic used to thunder past, now the pedestrian has right of way to wander from one souvenir shop to the next and explore cafés and restaurants. The spa hall, bathing beach, and spa park are all on the east bank of the lake.

Titisee-Neustadt Tourist Information Office
Strandbadstrasse 4
79822 Titisee-Neustadt
Tel. 07651 / 98 04 0
Fax 07651 / 98 04 40
Internet: www.titisee.de

2. Southern Black Forest
2.6 Donaueschingen, Hüfingen, Blumberg

The plateau separating the Black Forest from the Swabian Alb is called the **Baar.** Its flat, fertile landscape is mainly known for three things: the confluence of the rivers Brigach and Breg, the mansion of the Princes of Fürstenberg, and the annual meeting of the avant garde of modern music at the Donaueschingen Music Festival.

Generations of schoolchildren have learnt that "the Brigach and the Breg give rise to the Danube" (the Donau, in German), and the spring in the grounds of the Princes' mansion in Donaueschingen has always been regarded as its source. Indeed, the village of "Esginge" was given the name of "Donau-Eschingen" as long ago as the 13th century, and a 16th-century document registered the outflow from this spring as the "Danube rivulet".

Geographers usually define the source of this 2,773-kilometre long river as being the source of the Breg, as this is the longest tributary and the one with the greatest flow of water; it is in the middle of the Black Forest, near Martinskapelle, north of Furtwangen.

Donaueschingen people, nevertheless, assert that theirs is the true source; this is the point from which its length in kilometres is measured, and it is only from here that place-names include "an der Donau". In addition to this, Donaueschingen boasts a beautifully constructed setting for the "Donauquelle" spring, which draws many visitors every year. The mansion of the Fürstenberg Princes dates from 1772, and was given its present appearance in the 19th century. Visitors can enter it, and see the displays of costly porcelain and magnificent tapestries. The home of the princes is well known not only for the excellent

Fürstenberg beer brewed in the town; the Fürstenberg Archives, the Princes of Fürstenberg Collections, and a large number of baroque buildings in the town (which in 1908 survived a major fire unscathed) have also made the town famous.

The second floor of the Fürstenberg Collection building houses a gallery of paintings by the Swabian masters of the 15th and 16th centuries, and an Altar of the Passion and many other works by Hans Holbein the Elder.

The park gardens of the Princes' mansion in Donaueschingen, where the "source of the Danube" can also be found

 **Opening times for the Fürstenberg Collections**

Tuesday to Sunday, 9.00 am to 12.00 noon and 1.30 to 5.00 pm
Closed in November
Fürstenberg Mansion Museum
Only open to guided tours, from Easter to September
Every day except Tuesday, 9.00 am to 12.00 noon and 2.00 to 5.00 pm
Closed in the winter months.

The Donaueschingen Music Festival has been held almost every year since 1921. As a festival of contemporary music it has made a name for itself far beyond the borders of Germany, and draws musicians and music-lovers from all over the world.

Hüfingen, a small Black Forest town on the southern side of Donaueschingen, lies in the enchanting stretch of countryside stretching from the top of the Black Forest across the foothills of the Hotzenwald down to the Upper Rhine.

Even the ancient Romans felt themselves to be drawn as if by magic to the spot, in about 70 AD, to use the warm springs for their bath-houses. Today, Hüfingen has one of the best-preserved Roman baths in the whole of Europe and a museum documenting the age of the Romans. Römerzeit dokumentiert. An entirely different kind of charm is exercised by this small town on

Roman Baths Museum

**Guided tours by prior appointment
Not available in the winter.**

the Baar in spring: the colourful Hüfingen **Corpus Christi Festival** is one of the most traditional and colourful events in the Black Forest.

A colourful carpet of flowers for the Hüfingen Corpus Christi procession

Visitors who travel further south in the Black Forest will find in **Blumberg** the doorway to the big wide world.

Although the age of the great steam engines is over, a twisting section of railway line called the **Sauschwänzlebahn** between Blumberg and Stühlingen still has the old puffers travelling along it regularly.

A Sunday steam train on the "Sauschwänzlebahn"

This twisting stretch of track has a myriad of tunnels, valleys, and viaducts, and owes its name to the Swabian word for a pig's curly tail. The tightly curving tunnels, necessitated by the broken landscape, are now an attraction for the steam locomotive rides organised on Sundays from May to October.

As it was actually built for military purposes, this line is also called the "cannon line"; the general staff believed that a railway was needed for troop-transportation purposes that did not cross Swiss territory. However, the line never attained any military significance.

Nowadays, railway fans large and small storm into the historic carriages and wait excitedly for the train to reach the curving Weiler and Stockhalde tunnels; the line gains height by prescribing a 360°-curve inside the mountain.

Crossing the Wutach viaduct or the 264-metre long Epfenhofen viaduct are further highlights for technical enthusiasts.

Greetings from the station-master in the Blumberg museum office

This line almost met its end in 1955; it was taken out of service because it was no longer profitable, and falling to pieces as well. The armed forces then renovated it, again for strategic reasons, and in 1976 it should have been dismantled completely, but public-spirited Blumberg people and innumerable railway enthusiasts enabled it to start running historic trains again in 1977.

Timetable information on the Sauschwänzlein railway
Monday to Friday, 8.00 am to 12.00 noon
Tel. 07702 / 51200
Fax 07702 / 51222

2. Southern Black Forest
2.7 St. Peter, St. Märgen, Glottertal, Hexenlochmühle, Kandel, Waldkirch

The magnificence of the Black Forest can be enjoyed as a twin-pack from the sunny terrace of **St Peter.** Here, everything is that bit more magnificent and that bit bigger than elsewhere: the view, which can for instance be enjoyed on the twisty road between St Peter and St Märgen, or the monasteries that have stood in both towns for centuries, and of course the twin towers of the towns' churches. They are the landmarks of these two holiday towns, and visible from miles away.

St Peter is perhaps the better-known and livelier of the both towns. The Benedictine monastery was founded in the 11th century, and is the mausoleum of the Dukes of Zähringen. The present-day building in the middle of the little town with its bracing climate can be traced back to the 18th century; it was built in the baroque style between 1724 and 1757 to plans by the architect Peter Thumb.

The library hall is the high-point of baroque magnificence and architecture, its walls decorated with magnificent ceiling paintings and table paintings. In the curving gallery, statues representing the sciences watch over the library's treasures. The ceiling painting is the work of Benedikt Gambs (middle) and F.L. Herrmann.

Opening times for the former Benedictine Monastery of St Peter

Guided tours through Church and Monastery

Sundays and public holidays 11.30 am, Tuesday 11.00 am, Thursday 2.30 pm. and by prior appointment, Tel. 07660/91010

The characteristic double tours of the monastery church with their "onion" domes can be recognised from a long way away. The town is only half an hour by car from Freiburg, and its tourist season last all year round. In the summer, hiking and mountainbike paths coax day-visitors onto the sunny plateau with its view of the Feldberg, and in winter the ski-ers use the numerous Loipen leading from here all the way to Kandel or the Thurner cross-roads.

Hiking paths are cleared of excessive snow in winter, and Alpine ski-runs also entice day-visitors.

Recognisable from far away - the striking double tower of St Peter

The hiking paths and Loipen all meet together high above the town at a point known locally as the Potsdamer Platz, after the famous square in Berlin. A walk of only a few minutes leads to a small lake, the Plattensee, a popular destination for hikers well away from the beaten track.

On the other side of St Peter, heading into the valley of the little Dreisam river, a lovely walk takes the visitor across the sunny plateau of the Lindenberg chapel. The path leads along a former pilgrims' path, with Stations of the Cross. From the square in front of the little church one can enjoy a broad view out across the Zarten Basin of the Dreisam. For inhabitants of the Rhine valley escaping their eternal fogs, a view over the top of a sea of clouds is a very fine reward.

No less beautiful is the setting of **St Märgen,** reached by travelling along a twisting road with many fine views. This town has a natural bathing lake, and is a little closer to the grand back-drop of the Black Forest's highest peak, the Feldberg. The baroque church similarly once belonged to a monastery, and is surrounded by the buildings of a former abbey dating from the 12th century. It was dissolved in 1806, and its church became the parish church of St Mary. It had to be rebuilt after a fire in 1907, and now the Roman-style depiction of St Mary in the chapel is the destination of many a pilgrimage

As in the twin town of St Peter, there are excellent winter sports facilities available here: circular Loipen invited cross-country skiers to visit Hochwald or the Thurner, and there is also a lift for Alpine skiers. St Märgen also has a small chapel suitable as a destination for short excursions. On the Ohmen hill is the Judas Thaddäus chapel, to which the faithful made pilgrimages back in the Middle Ages. Another destination easily reached on foot is the Kapfenkapelle, on the edge of the forest; from above the town here one can see far across the mountain-top and even the Rhine valley.

The two monastery towns are linked by a twisty panorama road offering interesting views particularly from the section between St Peter and St Märgen and up to the Thurner. This holiday road runs from Waldkirch over the Thurner all the way to beyond Hinterzarten.

Between St Märgen and the Thurner, a well known cross-roads where there is an old hotel and a centre of Loipen, the road branches down into the Wilder Gutach valley. In the Hexenloch, a small deep valley only a few kilometres away from Furtwangen, there is one of the typical Black Forest water-mills in a particularly good state of preservation. Its characteristic double wheel makes the **Hexenlochmühle** one of the best-known water-mills in the Black Forest. Black Forest artefacts are on sale inside, and one can look at the great mill drive and look into the wood-working shop, where parts are made for cuckoo-clocks.

Anyone aiming for higher things leaves St Peter along the road heading towards **Glottertal.** After a few hairpin bends downwards, the road branches off to the **Kandel,** a bare mountain top 1,243 metres high which is a well known view point. Legend would have us believe it used to be the "Breisgau witches' dancing floor", but nowadays the visitor's attention is more likely to be drawn by hang-glider pilots starting from a ramp near the hotel and floating down into the Rhine valley.

The Kandel pyramid, which can be reached in only a few minutes from the car park, is one of the oldest viewing towers in the Black Forest. On clear days one can see all the way to the Kaiserstuhl and the Vosges, or southwards to the snow-covered peaks of the Alps.

Short, well signposted circular routes provide a walk round the summit, with ski-lifts on both sides of the road reaching up the gentle slopes. Children can often find a toboggan run here until well into the spring months on which they are safely well away from the Alpine skiers. This hill-top is usually free of fog in the autumn, and from **Waldkirch** it can be reached in about half an hour by car. Sometimes a weather situation prevails for days and weeks with colder air in the valleys than in the mountains, and the valley-dwells get depressed by the endless fog and escape to the sunlight uplands above Waldkirch.

This little town in the **Elztal** valley is a secret tip for any tour of the Black Forest. Here, on the edge of the Rhine valley, one can choose the best from both types of landscape. Down in the valley around the town there are gigantic strawberry fields, as well as vineyards.

The Black Forest and the Kandel on the one side, and the Kandel castle ruins on the other hand, are always in view even from the market square in the middle of this historic town.
sive church organ department. Many of the artistic mechanical hurdy-gurdies still preserved today, as well as church organs, originate from this town at the foot of the Kastelberg.

Every three years (e.g. in 1999) the finest examples return to their roots in the summer and enliven the Waldkirch Organ Festival. Other sights worth seeing in the Elztal museum are the collections of traditional local handicrafts. The Elztal Museum is housed in the town hall, and has an exten

**Opening times of the Elztal Museum
Tuesday to Saturday, 3.00 to 5.00 pm,
Sunday 11.00 am to 4.00 pm
November to Easter Saturday, Wednesday
and Friday, 3.00 to 5.00 pm,
Sunday 11.00 am to 4.00 pm.**

The polishers of precious stones who used the water from the Elz to driving their grinding-stones also have a long tradition behind them. Waldkirch also won fame with its new tourism strategy; the Elztal holiday experts offer "gentle holidays", with environmentally compatible offers from the region and for the region.

The Black Forest Zoo is a great hit with children. It covers about 12 acres, and does not house exotic animals from distant countries but mainly native species such as owls, stags, mountain goats, and racoons. The dwarf goats are without any doubt the most popular species.

The entrance to the Glottertal is another enchanting gateway for a journey into the Black Forest. It became famous when the television series "Black Forest Clinic" was filmed here, but the long, narrow village has retained its charms despite the flocks of visitors.
The State Insurance Institution's clinic was used for the hospital, and the house in which Professor Brinkmann lived was the "Hüsli" in Grafenhausen; other scenes in the film were produced at locations all over the Black Forest.

The inhabitants of the Glottertal valleys are proud of their wine. The grapes grow on the steep slopes at the entrance to the valley, and include the highest vineyards in Germany. "Roter Bur", the name of the wine-making co-operative and of its red wine, is based on the well known Spätburgunder grape grown here. A walk through the vineyards affords views down into the valley and out into the Rhine valley.

One of the most attractive gateways to the Black Forest - the Glottertal

The Glottertal is also well known for its hospitality and for its high-quality and sumptuous cuisine. In addition to numerous, more modern restaurants, the Goldener Engel in the middle of the village is perhaps the most striking: a fine wooden house next to the church in the main street, preserved with tender loving care. The Dilgerhof and Wuspenhof taverns are a little harder to find, and there is also a cheese factory on the edge of the village with its own cheese shop, offering dairy delicacies directly from the producer. The Hilzingen mill dates from 1621; it is an original, thatched mill, and can be reached from the upper end of the village on the right of the road leading towards St Peter. There is a great ceremony in the village to mark Corpus Christi, and the processions in Glottertal are amongst the most traditional and most beautiful in the Black Forest. Young and old are dressed in their finest traditional costume, and the young girls wear a glittering bejewelled head-dress called the "Rollenkranz". Numerous artistic pictures and carpets of flowers line the route of the procession.

3. The central Black Forest
3.1 Kinzigtal, Offenburg, Wolfach

The dukes of the Zähringen dynasty laid out their towns so logically and in such beautiful landscapes that every one of them is now a historical sight well worth seeing. The basic street-pattern of Offenburg is one of those with the typical Zähringen cross-shaped pattern, and has its two main axes running outwards to the four town gates. Offenburg has always been a centre of its region, for these reasons: its two main streets are old Roman roads, and it stands at the entrance to the **Kinzigtal** valley, one of the few natural routes through the Black Forest.

Offenburg today is a smart centre of administration, tourism, and business, notable for its position in the heart of the Ortenau region and at the entrance to the Black Forest. It was founded in 1148, and raised in 1235 to the rank of an Imperial city, beholden to the German Emperor alone. Its flourishing development came to a halt in 1689 when it was destroyed in the War of the Palatinate Succession.

The historic town centre, now almost entirely a pedestrian precinct, boasts many well preserved buildings. The baroque town hall, by the architect Matthias Fuchs, dates from 1741 and contains in its coat-of-arms an open gate symbolising the cosmopolitan, open-minded attitude of Offenburg people. The Austrian double eagle shows that the town has also been under Habsburg rule during the past 300 years. The museum in the town hall presents regional and industrial history.

**Opening times for the
Museum im Ritterhaus
Tuesday to Friday, 10.00 am to 1.00 pm
and 3.00 to 5.00 pm
Saturday and Sunday, 10.00 am to 5.00 pm**

It is not only historic buildings but also modern art in tangible form that Offenburg people offer their visitors. In the pedestrian precinct, in front of the town hall, stand the Vogelmenschen or "bird-people", life-size bronze sculptures on a rotating base by the Offenburg artists Ingrid and Dieter Werres; they invite young and old alike to "have a ride".

This is a good position from which to enjoy the town hall carillon. 25 bronze bells can play a repertoire of about 100 melodies. The Königshof, likewise in the town hall square, once housed the Ortenau administrative offices, and its fine façade still makes a great impression; the classic-style Salzhaus housed the "salt-measurer", back in the days when salt was as precious as gold.

In the main street, and the smaller ones leading off it, one will find a large number of well preserved patrician houses such as the Einhorn-Apotheke, a baroque building dating back to 1720 with its Neptune fountain (1783). Opposite the town hall is the fish market, with its lion fountain and the stepped gables of the Hirsch-Apotheke. Other sights worth seeing are the late baroque Beck'sche Haus and the grand Palais Battiany, both in Metzgerstrasse.

The brilliant baroque doorway of the Andreasspital in Spitalstrasse was rebuilt, like the rest of the building, in about 1700. The building near the fish-market was originally bestowed in aid of the poor and sick amongst Offenburg's citizens, and since it was renovated in 1982 exhibitions and special events have been held regularly in the former storage barn.

To the east of the main street, visitors interested in art will find a real treasure trove of baroque architecture in the former Franciscan convent in Lange Strasse. The convent is today the home of Augustine nuns.

The single-nave baroque church of Our Dear Lady was rebuilt in 1702 on gothic foundations and modelled on Vorarlberg churches. Its highlights include a richly decorated altar and a Silbermann organ. The graveyard chapel houses a fine 16th-century statue to the Virgin.

To the west of the main street is the Church of the Holy Cross. Franz Beer based its ground-plan, at the beginning of the 18th century, on the church in nearby Gengenbach. Only a few parts of its 13th-century gothic predecessor still remain.

The High Altar, the Renaissance crucifix, and the Sermon on the Mount group in front of the church are regarded as the most noteworthy sights in this parish church.

Offenburg today is known for trade fairs and publishing, but it nestles between the woods and the vineyards that stretch up from the Rhine valley far into the Kinzigtal and provide the three suburbs of Offenburg - Zell-Weierbach, Rammersweier, and Fessenbach - with their wine-growing industry and the city itself with the Ortenau Wine Festival. The village of Durbach is well known for its fruity Riesling wines, and together with a number of other wine-making villages lies "round the corner", a little way to the north of Offenburg.

The castle of Ortenberg stands at the point in the entrance to the Kinzigtal where the vineyards give way to the forest. These princely walls greet the traveller not as a ruin but as a carefully renov-ated and hospitable youth hostel, open to visitors of modest financial means. The Zähringen dukes built it in the 12th century to block the way into the Kinzigtal, but the French destroyed it in the 17th century. It was rebuilt in the neo-gothic style in 1838.

The little Kinzigtal town of **Gengenbach** has preserved its historic centre almost completely. Treating urban and domestic architecture with tender loving care has resulted in medieval and baroque buildings standing harmoniously alongside one another. A walk through this former imperial city gives one the impression that time has stood still.

Gengenbach's historic town centre

The **Museum of Rafting and Travel** welcomes the visitor at the entrance to the town; it is a former railway building now under a preservation order, and testifies to the importance of rafting (transporting tree-trunks as river rafts) and forestry in general, as well as showing the natural and corrected courses of the Kinzig

Opening times for the Museum of Rafting and Travel
April to October, Saturday, 2.00 to 5.00 pm
Sunday, 10.00 am to 12.00 noon
and 2.00 to 5.00 pm

river. The old town centre is dominated by historic half-timbered houses, richly decorated with flowers in the summer. The Kinzigtor and the Hohes Tor are the remaining representatives of three medieval town gates, and the classic-style town hall dates from the end of the 18th century. This massive building, which still totally dominates the market square and most of the town as well, was intended to document the self-confidence of the free imperial city in the face of the monastery.

The classic-style town hall dominates the market square of the former imperial city

The well preserved patrician houses all round the market square form an attractive back-drop. The Pfaffsches Haus on the western side once housed the council chancellery. The Löwenberg house on the south side now houses the **Museum of Local Arts and Crafts.** Towering over all of them is the Niggelturm, a tower now housing the **Narrenmuseum,** a museum of traditional Fasnet or carnival costumes and other items.

Opening times Gengenbach Museum of Local Arts and Crafts During special exhibitions Wednesday, 5.30 to 8.00 pm Saturday, 2.30 to 5.30 pm; Sunday, 10.00 am to 12.00 noon and 2.30 to 5.30 pm and also by appointment Narrenmuseum 1st April to 30th October, Saturday, 2.30 to 5.30 pm; Sunday, 10.00 am to 12.00 noon and 2.30 to 5.30 pm

Fragments remain of the towers that used to form part of the town walls. The best view of them all is from the Bergle, or Einbethenberg, a small hill with a medieval pilgrimage church on it directly in front of the town, by the river Kinzig. Even the Celts had a place of worship up here, and the Romans used it in honour of Jupiter.

The monastery close to the old town centre dates from the 18th century, when it was built on the foundations of a Benedictine monastery dating form the 8th century. The town first developed as dwellings huddled round the monastery, rising to the rank of an imperial city in 1218. Large parts of it were destroyed in the Thirty Years War, and the abbey took on its present-day appearance after that.

The Roman-style monastery church dates from the 12th century, and the present-day parish church is the result of many bouts of conversion work. The baroque treasures inside it include the choir stalls, the font, and the altar.

The Kinzigtal, a valley in which the Black Forest Railway and the main road run parallel with one another, narrows as one approaches its head, with side-valleys opening at regular intervals; at Biberach the Harmersbach valley leads to Zell and on to Bad Peterstal, with the Brandenkopf and the Geroldseck beckoning on either side as high vantage-points.

Haslach marks the start of the more difficult and therefore more attractive part of the Black Forest Railway; over the next 11 kilometres it will now have to climb 450 metres, passing through 36 tunnels on the way. In the **Black Forest Traditional Costume**

Museum, housed in a former Capucin monastery, one can trace the origins of the various types of costume, and find out why the ladies' traditional Bollenhut - a broad-brimmed black hat covered in huge red bobbles - has no right to appear in so many advertising pictures for the Black Forest; it is only actually worn in Gutach, Reichenbach, and Kirnbach, where it is traditionally part of the evangelical women's costume. It belongs in only three villages in the Gutach valley, where it is also still manufactured.

The Haslach town hall is decorated with historic wall-paintings

Opening times for the Black Forest Traditional Costume Museum

1st April to 31st October
Tuesday to Saturday, 9.00 am to 5.00 pm
Sunday and public holidays,
10.00 am to 5.00 pm; 1st November to 31st March, Tuesday to Friday, 9.00 am to 12.00 noon and 1.00 to 5.00 pm In January by prior appointment only

Hansjakob museum
Wednesday, 10.00 am to 12.00 noon and 3.00 to 5.00 pm 1st April to 31st October, also on Sunday, 10.00 am to 5.00 pm

The Hansjakob museum is housed in the Freihof, a gigantic Black Forest house with a broad, sloping roof. It houses mementoes of the writer, politician, and clergyman Dr Heinrich Hansjakob (1837 to 1916). The building was erected in 1912 as his retirement home, and became an old-people's home in 1916 and a museum in 1964. It also houses a permanent exhibition of works by the Haslach painters Carl Sandhaas, Louis Blum, and Otto Laible.

The basket market in front of Hausach railway station draws many visitors, and together with the Vogtsbauernhöfe open-air museum and the Dorotheen glass-works in Wolfach forms the local equivalent of the Bermuda triangle; visitors to the Black Forest admittedly do not disappear into it for ever, but they do seem to be drawn into it as if by magic.

The **Dorotheen glass-works** in Wolfach is a presentation-piece of ancient Black Forest artistry and craftsmanship. Here it is Christmas all year round: the extensive showrooms house not only glass decorations for the Christmas tree but also everything else that makes for a merry Christmas.

In the Dorotheenhütte in Wolfach one can watch the glass-blowers at work

Here, at the entrance to the Wolfachtal, one can find one of the most impressive glass-works in the Black Forest and watch craftsmen at their work. Anyone who would like to can try his or her hand and make an attractive container from the glowing gob of glass.

However, this glass-works is relatively young compared with the other branches of the local economy: it was wood-working, rafting, and mining that gave the town its importance. One can see something of its former splendour in the castle, through the gate of which one drives when leaving the town; it dates from the 17th century, and was the starting-off point for the Fürstenberg Princes in exercising their dominion over the northern Black Forest.

The little town of Wolfach lies at the confluence of the Wolfach and the Kinzig

Other sights worth seeing here are the 17th-century chapel and a small museum of local arts and crafts. There is a minerals museum in Oberwolfach, accommodated in a former farmhouse.

Opening times of the Bergbau- und Mineralienmuseum, Oberwolfach

May to October daily 11.00 am to 5.00 pm
December to April daily 2.00 to 5.00 pm

Closed in November

3. The Central Black Forest
3.2 Gutachtal, Vogtsbauernhof, Triberg

MITTEL

The **Gutachtal** is a genuine piece of the deepest Black Forest. The farmhouses are rarely as magnificent anywhere else but here, nor the forest darker, the sights more worth seeing or more numerous. In the relatively short valley between the opening into the Kinzigtal at **Hausach** and **Schönwald,** where the young Gutach flows down to the road connecting Furtwangen and Triberg, it is possible to experience the whole of the Black Forest in one small space.

The most impressive way of enjoying this landscape is from the train. The Gutachtal is the route of the Black Forest Railway, which passes through numerous tunnels, up to 1.7 kilometres in length, in order to work its way up into the mountains. A total of about 10 kilometres of the route from Hausach to St Georgen runs underground.

The engineer Robert Gerwig, who later also planned the Höllental railway between Freiburg and Hinterzarten, was commissioned in 1854 to plan the Black Forest railway. The 11-kilometre stretch between Hornberg and Sommerau must have been enough to give the engineers headaches on its own, as the railway has to climb a total height of 448 metres.

By 1866 the railway had been completed from Offenburg to Hausach, but then war interrupted the work, and the whole stretch from Offenburg to Villingen was not opened to traffic until 10th November 1873. Since then it has become a piece of German railway history.

Natural events kept giving the engineers problems. The workmen, many of them foreigner imported by the thousand for this difficult work, literally ran into granite, with the result that the originally planned route had to be given one or two extra tunnels in order to obviate immovable obstacles.

Natural events, in the form of landslides or heavy snow, also kept interrupting the operation of the railway. When travellers started taking a greater and greater interest in the Black Forest, detailed travel guides soon appeared offering useful tips for travelling on this railway.

As soon as one enters the Gutachtal from the north, one is invited to stay longer; no-one could drive straight past the **Vogtsbauernhöfe open-air museum,** where the finest Black Forest farmhouses have been brought together from all over the region.

The Vogtsbauernhof itself, the farmhouse from which the museum takes its name, dates from 1570 and was built on this site. The others have in some cases been carefully dismantled in order to save them from destruction and rebuilt here in the Gutachtal. This has created an impressive collection, which also reflects the regional characteristics of Black Forest architecture.

The initiator of this collection, Professor Hermann Schili, built the museum up during the period from 1963 to 1982, using seven basic forms of Black Forest farmhouse. All belong to the same basic type, but each was adapted to suit its local situation. And, of course, each was also extended to reflect the size and importance of the owner, who might have added a saw-mill or flour

Magnificent Black Forest farmhouses can be seen at the Vogtsbauernhof open-air museum

mill, a barn, a bake-house, or the so-called Leibgeding, the "old-folk's home" for the older generation.

The open-air museum is open to visitors from spring to late autumn, and numerous demonstrations of craftsmen's work take place in the individual houses.

Farmhouses are on display here, such as the Hotzenwald house and the Schauinsland house, that reflect totally different influences. The style of building gives an indication of the prosperity and influence of its owner and of the natural features to which it had to be adapted.

Opening times of the Vogtsbauernhöfe Open-Air Museum
1st April to 1st November
Every day from 8.30 am to 6.00 pm; last admission 5.00 pm

One feature common to all these farms is that they were built to live in with the materials available locally: wood, clay, and straw. They have been able to stand up to wind and weather for centuries without any very great maintenance work.

The deep, low roof is typical of this protective function. It gives the wind little space in purchase for an attack, and also keeps the outside walls almost completely dry even in gales and heavy rain.

Earlier generations were just as interested in conserving energy as we are, and housed their animals under the same roof as themselves in order to benefit from their warmth.

Farms like the Vogtsbauernhof are typical of the Gutachtal, and are only to be found around here. The stone wall of the main façade shows that this is Württemberg territory; kitchens had to be surrounded by stone walls, because of the risk of fire.

The Lorenzhof came from the Kinzigtal, where the climate is relatively mild. It is the oldest farmhouse in the museum, and was built in 1540.

The Hippenseppenhof, from the Furtwangen area, shows how practical-minded farmers were: in this farmhouse, as with many in the region, one can drive a horse and cart straight in under the roof.

However, this open-air museum is not just an assemblage of farmhouses, but a museum that lives. On summer days, in particular, the site throbs with the flood of visitors. Ancient hand crafts are demonstrated in many of the houses, or else one can simply see how the ingenious farmers of hundreds of years ago solved the problems of everyday life.

There are bake-houses and distilleries, which were just as much a necessity of life in these remote farmhouses as were their own tiny chapels.

The grain was ground in their mills, and the "Kleiekotzer" - a mask designed to ward off evil spirits from the daily bread - is on display, as are the gigantic millstones or the jumble of drive-belts that drove the machines.

Black Forest cloth used to be woven on huge wooden looms

The water power of Black Forest streams used to drive the heavy mill-wheels

Many farmhouses needed a saw-mill, and hemp-grinding and marker stones are also items of use from an almost forgotten daily life on the farm.

Many visitors, however, are particularly interested to see how life was conducted inside these mass-ive farmhouses, and hardly any question goes unanswered. Everything is present, from the beds (far too small for present-day people) to the wooden knives and forks, many of which the farming people had to make for themselves.

Some details almost seem mystical, and hard for the visitor to discover without a knowledgeable guide or a good guide-book. Devil-knots and witches' knots are carved into the wood in certain places, again to ward off evil spirits.

If the smoke rose upwards and the kitchen were often pitch black, this did not mean that the farmer's wife had no great feeling for cleanliness. The smoke helped to prevent pests from nesting in the structure, and also to preserve the buildings for centuries.

Every visitor should definitely leave plenty of time for a visit to this museum. In addition to looking round the houses, there are demonstrations of traditional crafts, groups to admire in traditional costume, and plenty of opportunities to sit and rest.

There is an old German phrase for a grand event deteriorating into a laughable flop, "the whole thing ended up like the **Hornberg cannonade",** which only historians can explain, but which is demonstrated every year in the small Gutachtal town of **Hornberg.**

An open-air stage is set up, and every year since 1955 the town's Historical Association has reenacted the debacle that made the town so famous.

It is all supposed to have happened in 1564, when the citizens were preparing to receive the Duke of Württemberg with a guard of honour and 21-gun salute.

All men of military age and all the militias of the surrounding area came together, and a watchman was placed on the top of the castle tower to spot the guest-of-honour from far away and warn the yeomanry below.

The Hornberg cannonade is re-enacted at the open-air festival

When the watchman called out that the Duke was coming, all the guns were let off in his honour - but it proved to be a false alarm. Then the sentry called his warning again - also a false alarm. And by the time the Duke actually did arrive, the Hornberg militia had fired off all its gunpowder, and the only salute it could give was to shout "bang-bang" as loudly as possible.

There are in fact two castles towering over the valley, the Lower Castle and the Althornberg. The Black Forest railway crosses the river here with a massive viaduct, and the lively Historical Association dedicated a fountain to it in 1955. The story of the "Hornberg cannonade" became well known mainly through Schiller's play "Die Räuber", where the comparison was made for the first time.

Between Hornberg and **Triberg,** the Black Forest Railway runs through its longest tunnel. Anyone alighting at Triberg is welcomed by a cuckoo - metaphorically, at least, as the Gutachtal is the heart of the old clocks and watches industry. Shops selling cuckoo-clocks are of course to be found all over the Black Forest, but here there is probably the greatest concentration of firms making these hand-carved high-precision instruments.

The **Triberg waterfall** can be reached in just a few minutes from the town centre. Here the Gutach cascades down from the conf-fluence of the Weissenbach and the Schwarzenbach over a total of seven waterfalls and a drop of 160 metres. When the snows are melting, the water roars in clouds over the huge granite blocks, and even at quieter times of year it creates an impressive background noise.

The scenery all around is also impressive. Surrounded by thick woods, undisturbed by busy roads, one can climb a zig-zag path to the top of the waterfall - a stiff climb, for which one should allow at least an hour to the top and back.

Triberg also offers its guests a fine selection of restaurants, for instance the Parkhotel Wehrle. The pilgrimage church of "St Mary in the pine-tree", with its baroque interior, and the interesting museum of local arts and crafts are further sights well worth seeing in the town.

The outstanding attraction in Triberg is the „Black Forest Museum" with its large collection of clocks. It is one of the most visited museums of local history and culture in Germany with exhibits displayed over 1.600 m2 of floor space featuring a collection of Black Forest tradition and Europe´s largest collection of barrel organs - both well worth seeing and hearing. A visit to the museum in Triberg promises a brief encounter with the Black Forest´s past.

3. The central Black Forest
3.3 Furtwangen

The best approach to **Furtwangen** is on foot, from the north-west, because the source of the Danube is only a short distance away, on a hill called the Brend, right in the middle of the Black Forest. Compared with the glamour that Donaueschingen has enjoyed for centuries, with the fine spring in the grounds of the Princes' mansion marking the source of the Danube, this little spring on the Brend, above Martinskapelle, seems more like a dreamy little brook.

You can stand here and place your hand on an imaginary line running through the whole of Europe, the principal watershed.

You could send a tree-leaf floating down the Danube all the way to the Black Sea, or walk a short distance to the west, to the source of the Elz, and taste a sip of the clear spring water that flows, after a rather shorter journey, into the North Sea.

The hills around Furtwangen are ideally suitable for seeing the Black Forest from its best side. The historic tavern of Martinskapelle was once a fine 15th-century farmhouse, rebuilt in 1739 using the old timber a second time.

Martinskapelle is now the centre of an extensive network of Loipen, and has contributed to establishing Furtwangen as a winter sports centre not restricted to Alpine ski-ing.

This area is a miniature paradise for hikers, with its intersecting long-distance hiking paths and many circular routes, perfected by a number of fine old taverns and the viewing tower on top of the Brend.

Somewhat modest in appearance, the concrete tower offers a fine view from an altitude of 1149 metres over the gently rolling central Black Forest, and belongs on any list of fine viewing-points.

The hotel of the same name offers a pleasant stay on the Brend. There has been a ski hut directly below the tower since 1905 which developed long ago into a popular tavern for day-visitors.

Furtwangen is an education town of semi-national significance, and particularly for the clock-making industry. Near the College of Advanced Technology in the middle of the town is the **Clock Museum,** opened in its present form in 1992 and probably unique in Germany. Everything is represented here, from antique chronometers to ultra-modern time-measuring instrumentation, from the miniature pocket-watch to a mechanism big enough to fill a room.

However, the museum does not just display this range of clocks and watches but also demonstrates the importance and the artistic skill of this traditional craft. Old clock-makers' workshops have been set up in the modern rooms, and a collection of cuckoo-clocks and other wooden Black Forest clocks shows the possibilities this raw material offered in the early phases of industrialisation.

Hans Lang's artistic astronomical clock

Shield clocks may not be as well known as cuckoo-clocks, but they are almost as important. The shields were often made by specialist painters in their home workshops.

A Black Forest clock workshop, and early Black Forest clocks

The people who planned the Furtwangen museum have produced a collection not only of the traditional, local clocks which formed the foundation of the clock-making industry here but also valuable pieces from all over the world: baroque pendulum clocks, or musical-boxes, for instance, in which the mechanism is connected to a whole group of miniature musicians playing their instruments.

The museum originated from the Furtwangen clock-making school of the Archdukes of Baden, and today the museum houses the greatest historical collection of clocks and watches. The first collection was established and opened to the public as long ago as 1852; its present form dates from 1992, since when it has enjoyed the enormous interest of visitors.

Furtwangen is therefore the high-point of a journey along the German Clock Road.

Opening times for the German Clock Museum

1st April to 31st October, every day, 9.00 am to 6.00 pm
1st November to 31st March, every day, 10.00 am to 5.00 pm

3. The central Black Forest
3.4 St. Georgen, Schramberg, Villingen, Schwenningen

The towns in the central Black Forest lie on a plateau on the edge of the Baar as if on a silver salver. The one in the centre is in fact the double city of **Villingen-Schwenningen**, which has developed into the centre of the region; non-identical twins, Villingen with its historic town centre and Schwenningen more the small, modern industrial town.

Bird´s eye view of the historical town centre of Villingen

Here, 700 metres above sea level, the visitor is surrounded by the leisure facilities of the Baar and its two adjoining regions, the Black Forest and the Swabian Alb, with a network of about 300 kilometres of hiking paths and 100 kilometres of Loipen in the winter.

Villingen was founded by the Zähringen dynasty, and is a well preserved collection of medieval buildings. Alemannic tribes setled here as long ago as the 6th century, and in the 11th the Zähringen dynasty ruled the town; in 1218 it became an imperial city.

It grew rapidly in the 13th century, and even a few monasteries settled here. Like many Black For-est towns, however, Villingen also has Austrian roots, and a connection with the Archdukes of Baden, the legacy of which is its beautiful historic town centre surrounded by a defensive wall.

The typical Zähringen cross-shaped town plan has also been preserved, and many patrician houses. In the centre is the Minster of Our Dear Lady, the 12th-century Catholic parish church with a Roman-style nave and gothic towers; its interior harbours valuable church treasures such as a silver disc cross and a golden Fürstenberg chalice.

The fountain in the square behind the Minster is witty and modern, with numerous details, original figures, and a bronze tower bearing inscriptions, inviting the visitor to spend a long time looking at it.

The old town hall is a late gothic, three-storey building in Rathausgasse which has also served since 1876 as a museum of municipal history and for exhibitions.

The new town hall, which is allegedly in fact older than the old one, stands in the square behind the Minster, a gothic building once the home of the Minster clergy.

The fountain in the Minster square narrates the history of the town

Opening times for the Altes Rathaus museum

on request, Tel. 07721/822351

The Romäusturm is a tower commemorating the popular hero Romäus Mans, who is said to have transported the great town gate from Rottweil to Villingen in the 15th century. In the Franciscan Museum in Rietgasse one can gain an insight into the former monastery and see pieces from the Fürstenberg mau-

Opening hours of the Franciscan Museum
Tuesday to Saturday 10.00 am to 12.00 noon
and 1.00 to 5.00 pm
Sunday and public holidays 1.00 to 5.00 pm

Cafe in the museum,
Tuesday to Sunday 10.00 am to 5.00 pm

soleum of Magdalenenberg. No-one can fail to notice another fountain, the Radmacherbrunnen, in the pedestrian precinct. It commemorates a wager which a carter won in 1562 by driving a wheel to Rottweil and back in one day. And this town has to have a Narrenbrunnen, as Villingen is one of the strongholds of the Alemannic-Swabian Fasnet tradition - a mixture of Rhineland carnival and Celtic spring rites.

The neighbouring town of Schwenningen was first mentioned in historical records in 817 AD, and was raised in 1140 to a Zähringen town with its own law-court. It competed for a long time against Villingen, but in 1633, at the height of the Thirty Years War, it was burnt to a cinder. It regained its status as a town in 1907, and in the 1920s and 1930s was the world's biggest city for clocks and watches; these, together with shoe fac-

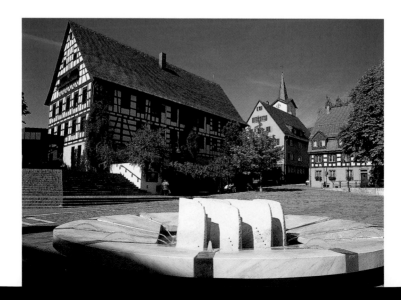

tories, had brought it an economic boom at the beginning of the century. The Clock-Making Industry Museum, in a historic building which started life as the first Württemberg clock factory, invites the visitor in. Another museum of clocks and watches in housed in a farmhouse dating from 1697, at Kronenstrasse 16, and shows the history of clock-making and the development of this branch of industry. The production of pendulum clocks can also be followed in the Museum of Local Arts and Crafts and Clocks, together with the history of Black Forest glass-making.

A point of attraction for guests who enjoy the water is the spa town of **Bad Dürrheim,** with its brine spa baths - the only one of its kind in the Black Forest. Deep shafts bring to the surface the "white gold" which was discovered in 1822. Brine baths were on offer here as early as 1851 - but in wooden tubs. The little lake, Salinensee, offers boating in the summer and skating in the winter. The Narrenschopf is a museum in the Luisenpark displaying 400 figures in the Narren (clown or jester) costume worn for Fasnet.

St Georgen is the highest point along the Black Forest Railway; from there south-eastwards it runs downwards all the way to Lake Constance. St Georgen is also the starting-point of a long-distance hiking path, the Black Forest / Jura / Lake Constance route, which covers a distance of 112 kilometres to Radolfzell and is one of the great hiking paths of the Black Forest. But why would anyone want to wander so far away? - St Georgen numerous attractions, and not only its leisure facilities and a bracing climate (its altitude is between 800 and 1,000 metres). For instance, the Benedictine monastery at the source of the Breg was founded in 1094.

To return to more recent history, "Dual" gramophones were manufactured here over a period of many years. However, the age of CD-players and Far Eastern production methods has left

Opening times of the Fasnet Museum	
1st May - 31st Oct.	1st Nov. - 30th April
Mon. to Sat. 2 to 5.30 pm Sun. and public holid. 10.00 am to 5.30 pm	Mon. to Sat. 2 to 5 pm Sun. and public holid. 10.00 am to 5.00 pm

Museum of Local Arts, Crafts and Gramophones
Monday to Friday, 9.00 am to 12.30 pm and
2.00 to 5.00 pm (6.00 pm on Thursdays)
Saturdays from May to September, 10.00 am to
12.00 noon Closed on Sunday and public holiday

the town with nothing more than a Museum of Local Arts and Crafts and Gramophones to remind visitors of an industry which was once the biggest employer in the region.

Anyone who is only looking for rest and relaxation should spend time at the Klosterweiher natural bathing beach, where it is also possible to hire a boat. There is a natural skating rink in the winter. The Stadtfest, on the first weekend in July, and the Seenachtfest are among the high-points of the year. The Black Forest Railway is not the only way of reaching the lower levels of the Black Forest from St Georgen. Another line of development is the **Schiltach** valley, which starts near here and leads first to the castle town of Schramberg before opening up into five separate valleys.

Erhard Junghans founded the clock-making industry here in 1860, and by the turn of the century Schramberg boasted one of the biggest clock and watch factories in the world. However, times goes by differently in the Far East, and the quartz-controlled time-measurer superseded the labour-intensive mechanical clock, with the result that many jobs were lost.

**Opening times for Schramberg
town museum
Tuesday to Friday,
2.00 to 6.00 pm
1st May to 15th September
also 10.00 am to 12.00 noon
Saturday and Sunday, 10.00 am to 12.00
noon and 2.00 to 5.00 pm**

There is a collection of Black Forest clocks in the town museum, which also displays the life and times of the Junghans clock factory. For a long time, rafting (sending tree-trunks downstream as rafts) also played an important role, but today this Black Forest community is best known to the Narren - those who celebrate Carnival riotously, in full costume - in southern Germany. The traditional "Da-Bach-na-Fahrt" spectacle draws many thousands of spectators in the Fasnet season every year. Travelling in old-fashioned washing tubs, and more modern but just as crazy vehicles, the revellers travel about 500 metres down to the Schiltach between dense crowds of spectators - and, of course, usually end up with a good wetting. To ensure that they survive the plunge into the icy water, these dare-devil drivers need two good shots of Schnaps before they start and two more when they have been fished out of the river. Three ruined castles bear witness to the former greatness of **Schramberg.** Art-lovers travel on a little further, in the direction of the village of Buchenberg, just before which one arrives at the ruined castle of Waldau, from where one can see the former litt le St Nikolaus church. It dates from the 12th century, was enlarged in the 15th century, and possesses a rich interior from those days, including wall paintings

Schramberg, the town of clocks

Schramberg's town hall is in a central location

and a font stone. The drive along the Schiltachtal will be rewarded with a view of the medieval town centre of Schiltach. Half-timbered houses and cobbled alleys huddle round the steeply sloping market square. The old town centre, its renaissance town hall, and the old market fountain are under preservation orders. Anyone who would like to explore the old town below the castle ruins should wander along the narrow alleys and up and down the Stäffele - steep, narrow flights of steps. In the middle of the town, directly alongside the river, is a traditional leather-tannery where one can also buy hides and leather articles.

3. The central Black Forest
3.5 Rottweil

For 11 months of the year, the Neckar town of **Rottweil** slumbers away happily. People go about their business, visitors set out from here to explore the Black Forest, and the streets are as clean and tidy as the Swabians here would expect.

But then comes the "fifth season", known as Carnival in the Rhineland and Fasnet here, and the whole town goes mad. The Narrensprung, the spectacular procession of the Narren (carnival clowns) in Rottweil, is just the visible tip of a total crazy iceberg. People who live in Rottweil, and many more who would like to, do not make any hard and fast plans for the Alemannic Fasnet, the mad days from "Smutzige Dunschtig" (the last Thursday before Lent begins) and Ash Wednesday.

The Narrensprung is the high-point of antics of the Rottweil carnival clowns

Instead, they take time off from work because they know that, for these few days, nothing is poss-ible except the antics of the Narren. Anyone who really wants to enjoy it all has to get up early; punctually, at 8.00 am on Rosenmontag (the Monday before Shrove Tuesday) some 3,000 of these clowns and jesters stream out of the town through its best-known gate, the Schwarzes Tor. "Schantle" and "Federahannes" caper around the town centre before the eyes of up to 30,000 spectators, many of whom have travelled a long way to be here. The spectacle is repeated at 8.00 am and 2.00 pm the next day, before the Narren disappear again until next year. This highly traditional activity actually has nothing to do with the merry-making further down the Rhine or the Fasching (carnival) festivities in Cologne, with their traditions of joking and singing and swinging. The marches to which the Narren march have remained unchanged for centuries, and the Kleidle, the clothes they wear, are also based on very old traditions; here again, no new-fangled innovations are ever permitted. All these fun and games are taken extremely seriously. The tradition is preserved by a Narrenrat, or Council of Clowns. Whilst in other towns new groups are formed every year to parade in new costumes, a Narrenkleiderrat (clown-costume council) watches sternly to ensure that the tradit-ional forms are retained.

Of course, this former imperial city on the banks of the Neckar has plenty to offer at other times of year as well. Rottweil people have not only successfully retained their traditions and protected them from harmful outside influences, but have also done the same for the heart of their town. It is graced by medieval houses dating from the 14th and 15th centuries, and patrician houses from the Renaissance and baroque periods.Renaissance und dem Barock.

Well preserved - Rottweil's medieval town centre

Rottweil is, as far has historians can tell, the oldest town in Baden-Württemberg; the Romans established a settlement here in 74 AD at the point where the roads from Straßburg to Augsburg and from Switzerland to Rottenburg meet, and called it arae flaviae, the predecessor of Rottweil.

The presence of salt no doubt also helped the town to gain its prominence; this was a valuable commodity in the Middle Ages. The visitor can find out more about these once precious crystals in the Unteres Bohrhaus brine museum.

Opening times of the Brine Museum
1st May to 30th September
Sundays, public holidays, 2.30 to 5.00 pm
Individual guided tours by prior
appointment

The historic centre of the town also reveals its history. If one turns left at the corner of the town hall instead of following the main road down to the Neckar, one arrives at the Minster of the Holy Cross, a gothic church rebuilt in the 16th century.

The former imperial city on the Neckar marks the frontier of the Black Forest

The Rottweil town museum in the main street shows everyday culture in Rottweil between 1750 and 1870, and also a model of the imperial city as it would have appeared in the later Middle Ages. The Dominican Museum in Kriegsdamm is a branch of the Württtemberg State Museum in Stuttgart, and its exhibits include finds from Roman times, wooden sculptures, and various travelling exhibitions. Further out of town, close to the town walls, is the Lorenzkapelle, a former chapel now housing the Museum of Masonry.

Another sight worth seeing is the 70-metre high tower of the chapel church, regarded as an example of the flamboyant style. The three doorways are well preserved of the church which was built in 1340, and has a gothic exterior and a baroque interior. Anyone visiting here for more worldly pleasures should try the Aquasol brine baths, or walk to the Neckarburg castle ruins. It was first mentioned in historical documents in 763 AD, but has not been inhabited since the 17th century.

Visible from far and wide - the tower of the chapel church

Opening times
Town Museum
Tuesday to Saturday, 10.00 am to 12.00 noon and 2.00 to 5.00 pm
Sunday, 10.00 am to 12.00 noon
Dominican Museum
Tuesday to Sunday, 10.00 am to 12.00 noon and 2.00 to 5.00 pm
Museum of Masonry
Tuesday to Sunday, 2.00 to 5.00 pm

3. The central Black Forest
3.6 Alpirsbach, Dornstetten, Freudenstadt, Baiersbronn, Waldachtal, Altensteig

The name of **Alpirsbach,** at the top of the Kinzigtal, means something to many people: some think of the monastery, others more readily of the well known brewery. And then there is the large number of hikers and winter-sports holiday-makers who connect the name with broad coniferous forests and magnificent Loipen.

The visitor's first port of call is the middle of the picturesque town, which rose to prosperity long before the brewery was built. It is dominated by the monastery church of the former Benedictine abbey, which no-one can miss; its red sandstone can be seen from far away above the gables of the town.

The lords of the houses of Zollern, Sulz, and Hausen endowed this monastery at the end of the 11th century. Parts of it were destroyed by fire at the beginning of the 16th century, and plundering peas-ants quite often raided the abbey.

Duke Ulrich of Württemberg dissolved the monastery in 1535 and turned into a Latin (grammar) school. Today the monastery houses not only the Evangelical parish church in the former

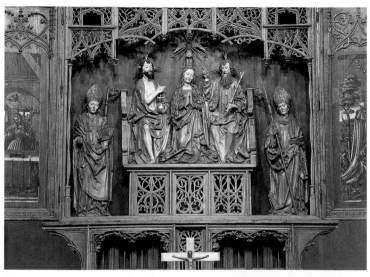

The altar of the former monastery church in Alpirsbach

refectory but also provides space for Catholic services and a monastery museum. The church is regarded as the most important Roman-style building in the Black Forest. The Roman-style lower floor of the church carries a gothic Choir. The upper part of the tower and the stepped gable date from the 15th and 16th centuries.

A visitor entering through the west door arrives first in an anteroom with three arcades. An inscription runs round the west door: "I am the gate, spake the Lord, and he who enters through Me shall be blessed", an invitation to all visitors engraved in stone. The interior of the church makes a very austere impression; one notices the influence of the Hirsau school, and the Benedictine feeling for the monumental. The only decoration in this ante-room is a bas-relief of Christ. If one looks back from the Choir through the crossing into the nave, one can see clearly the forbidding austerity of the architecture. Not much is left of the Roman-style interior except the hinges on the west doors and the 14th-century choir stalls. The monastery church is open to visitors between services as well, and there are guided tours. The town centre offers an opportunity for a quiet stroll through the old town.

The brewery itself is not open to visitors, although one can see the filling lines. The Alpirsbach gallery, with varying art exhibitions, and the glass-blowing works at Krähenbadstrasse 3 are in the hands of the monastery brewery, which has also set up a small brewery museum. The Museum of Municipal History in Ambrosius-Blarer-Platz is accommodated in rooms that originally belonged to the monastery, and shows the history of the town and the monastery. In the suburb of Reinerzau there is a dam across the baby Kinzig.

Dornstetten is one of the oldest towns in the Black Forest mountains, set 700 metres above sea level on a ridge between the

 Opening times for the Museum of Municipal History
Easter until early November
Thursday, Saturday, Sunday, and
public holidays, 2.00 to 5.30 pm
and by prior appointment

Murgtal and the Glattal. The town centre boasts a smart market square with a fountain, surrounded by half-timbered cottages

and medieval town defences. The Black Forest landscape changes here; to the east, the Heckengäu and the Schlehengau are quieter, more tranquil areas. The suburb of Aach contains the oldest hotel in the northern Black Forest, a half-timbered building 425 years old and still preserved in almost its original state.

The monastery buildings dominate the town

It is now only a few kilometres to **Freudenstadt,** the nodal point on the high Black Forest plateau. This is the starting-point of the Black Forest High Road, the road along the top of the Black Forest, and its first and most important holiday road, and also the point where the Black Forest Valleys Road and the Black Forest Baths Road intersect. The town was built in the 17th century at the instigation of Duke Friedrich of Württemberg, who wanted to give new impetus to his nearby Christophstal silver mine and also to defend the pass at Kniebis. This was the origin

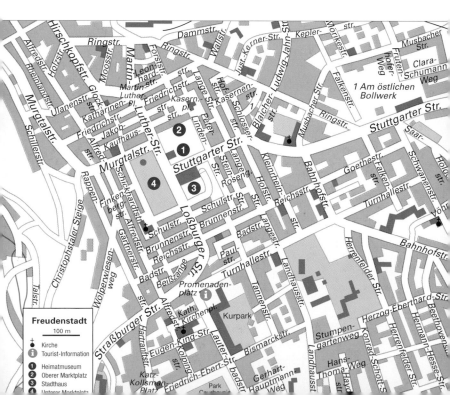

of the chess-board like town plan, with a gigantic market square (literally square in shape) in the middle. The palace that was originally to have been built in the middle of the square was never even started.

The town was burnt down in 1945, but then completely rebuilt and given its new and striking appearance. The town centre is still arranged as one square set of streets within another around the market square that forms the heart of this tourist town.

The market square has a side-length of 225 metres, making it the biggest in Germany. It was successfully redesigned in the 1990s, with the parked cars mainly disappearing underground.

Freudenstadt's market square and strictly geometrical town centre

The charming arcaded walks with their many attractive shops all round the square invite the visitor to stroll and window-shop.

If anyone finds the market square and the town centre too big for a pleasant walk can step aboard the little railway train, the Kurbähnle, which still makes its rounds every summer and is usually packed full.

The town hall is located on the square, with a museum of local arts and crafts, a collection which bears witness to old hand crafts and to the history of the town.

There are special points of attraction at two of the corners of the market square. One is the town hall, a relatively young building built like so many others in the years after the war, and dominating the square with its tower.

Opposite, on the quieter side of the square, the Evangelical town church stands alongside a small park.

At the beginning of the 17th century, Heinrich Schickhardt built the church in the form of an angle round this corner. The interior is also dominated by the right-angle, with the congregation looking towards the altar from two directions.

For a long time, this division was used as a way of strictly segregating the sexes during services.

The 16th-century crucifix and the early 12th-century font have been preserved from the once rich interior. The best-known item is the 12th-century Roman-style reading desk with the four evan-

Arcades all round the market square invite the visit to stroll and window-shop

gelists; it is believed to have come originally from Alpirsbach.

The town on its plateau is surrounded by a network of hiking paths and Loipen. There are boats for hire on the Langwaldsee in the town park, and on the hill next to the town, the Kienberg, is the Friedrichsturm (1899). A walk along the Christophstal, in which miners once used to work, brings the visitor to a small mansion called the Bärenschlössle (1627).

The panorama bath on the hills above the town was designed particularly for winter pleasure. One can sit in the warm water and allow one's gaze to wander out across the thick forests of the surrounding area, and to pour heat back into one's veins after the joys of winter sports.

The name of the village of Baiersbronn sounds like music in the ears of gourmets. When the new restaurant guides appear every year, **Baiersbronn** always takes an extraordinarily high position, high at least in relation to the small size and remote position of the village. The restaurateurs are given good marks by all the testers, and gourmets come from far and wide to visit the fine kitchens in Baiersbronn. The village also scores well in the statistics for visitors staying overnight, with an annual figure in the millions. This is not only due to the delightful surroundings but also to the fact that Baiersbronn is in fact a collection of ten small

Baiersbronn, the gourmet's Mecca

towns, and is a spa town with as many beds for visitors as for its own inhabitants. Baiersbronn holds another record: the municipality with the largest area of woodland in Germany. Out of a total area of 19,000 hectares, 16,000 are covered in forest. It is an outstandingly suitable place from which to start numerous excursions, as one can reach the Nagoldtal just as easily as the Murgtal. Four lakes are also within easy reach, beside the High Road and where the upper reaches of the Nagold run into an artificial lake.

The idyllic Huzenbach lake, in the village of the same name, is reputed by legend to be full of nixes, marsh-women, and other elves and fairies. Anyone who releases a goblin from its spell can be sure of a reward. One way of reaching the lake is along a hiking route eight kilometres long. Three kilometres south of Baiersbronn, the Senkbach waterfalls crash down into the valley near the Murg.

North of Baiersbronn, in Heselbach, is the former woodland chapel of Reichenbach monastery. The monastery church of St George in Kosterreichenbach dates back to an endowment made in 1082 which allowed the monastery of Hirsau to found its first Benedictine patronage. The "Grosse Tannen" Nature Park, near Pfalzgrafenweiler, shows how the forests would have originally appeared all around Freudenstadt. The tallest pines in the whole of the Black Forest stand in the village of Kälberbronn, on a plateau between the nature conservancy area of Zinsbachtal

The various parts of Baiersbronn are scattered over a wide area

and the Waldachtal; some of them are 50 metres tall, and up to 250 years old. 70 percent of the whole area of this municipality consists of high-level forest.

Waldachtal is a small town with park lakes and an old saw-mill on the edge of the Black Forest, where it borders with the Neckarland. The pilgrimage church of Heiligbronn dates from 1750. However, one only needs to travel a few kilometres further down into the Nagold valley to be once again in the depths of the Black Forest.

The picturesque town of Altensteig, on the upper reaches of the Nagold, lies on a steep hill crowned by a castle and a church. The whole medieval collection is best viewed by approaching the town along the road from Egenhausen. The view of this little old Swabian town can be enjoyed on a walk through its narrow alleys, up and down steep steps, through the higgledy-piggledy collection of half-timbered buildings and ancient walls.

Opening times for the Municipal and Fire-Brigade Museum

Wednesday, 2.00 to 4.00 pm
Sunday, 11.00 am to 12.00 noon
and 2.00 to 4.00 pm
but May to September until 5.00 pm
Groups also by prior appointment

The castle dates from the 11th century, and its present-day appearance is basically late gothic. The old castle now houses the municipal and fire-brigade museum.

The Evangelical parish church (1775) lies only a little way away, on a hill above the town. There is also a castle in the village of Berneck, built by the Barons of Gültlingen; it dates from the 12th century, with its protective walls and battlements, but the interior is not open to the public.

In the village of Altensteigsdorf, the wall-paintings in the late Roman-style Choir tower of the Evangelical parish church has only been preserved to a modest extent. Remains can also be seen of more recent paintings.

4. Northern Black Forest
4.1 Black Forest High Road
Freudenstadt to Baden Baden, Bad Peterstal, Griesbach Bühlerhöhe, Rippoldsau, Schappach, Mummelsee, Kloster Allerheiligen

The **Black Forest High Road** is one of the most brilliant tourist attractions in the Black Forest. It runs from Freudenstadt to Baden-Baden, along the ridge of the wooded hills, and as the first tourist road in the State was intended to show holiday-makers the beauty of the region. Tourism has developed further, but this holiday road has lost nothing of its significance.

The Black Forest High Road is not only successful because of the sights worth seeing directly on either side of it, but because it forms the basis for a large number of possible short excursions which one can make well away from the main route, in order to discover the Black Forest from its quiet side.

Shortly after leaving Freudenstadt one reaches the Kniebis, 980 metres above sea level and one of the high-points of the whole route. This old Black Forest pass was always strategically important, as can be seen from the Schwedenschanze fortress, built by the Swedes during the Thirty Years War, and its counterpart the Schwabenschanze.

Not far beyond the **Kniebis,** one can branch off the main route down towards **Bad Peterstal-Griesbach.** This is a spa town with health-giving mineral and mud baths, deep in the valley of the Rench, and famous for the power of its springs, which are used for baths and as mineral water.
The invigorating effect of the mineral water, with its high carbon-dioxide content, was already being put to good use in the 14th century. The ski-jump high above the town is the venue not only for competitions in the winter, when one can watch the dare-devils flying straight at the village, but also for summer ski-jumping.

Health-holidays started in Griesbach back in the 16th century. The main town in the upper Rench valley is Oppenau, founded originally on account of the former **Kloster Allerheiligen** ("Monastery of All Saints") far above it, near the High Road.

Here in the Lierbachtal, just below the 1055-metre high Schliffkopf, Duchess Uta von Schauenburg founded a Prémontré convent in the 12th century. An excursion there on foot is worthwhile if only for the All Saints waterfalls, which cascade down about 100 metres into the valley. A small footpath leads via a flight of steps past the waterfalls and on to the rest of the convent buildings.

The remains of the walls of the former All Saints

On can then return to the High Road, which runs across a broad plateau between the Kniebis and here. The typical hills are called Grinden, soft, rounded peaks which are the counterparts to the "Balloons" of Alsace.

The upland marshes, caused here by the high level of rainfall and the imperviousness of the soil, have now mainly been drained, but one exception worth seeing is the Wildsee, 2,5 kilometres from the top of the pass at Ruhestein.

From Euting-Grab, on the footpath to the bank of the lake, one can look down on the small, circular lake surrounded by cliffs up to 115 metres high. The path down to the lake is steep. Anyone who stays up on the heights will soon arrive at the Darmstädter Hütte, and savour a little of true hiking atmosphere.

A hiking route on the other side of the Black Forest High Road promises a very special adventure. Anyone who walks from Ruhestein towards the Rhine valley will soon run into the Karlsruhe Ridge. This Alpine climb is not exactly suitable for a Sunday afternoon stroll; it makes demands even on experienced hikers and mountaineers, and should not be tackled without the right equipment.

The sights worth seeing along the High Road are strung along it like a pearl necklace, with the centre of focus being the **Mummelsee,** the highest lake (1,032 metres above sea level) in the whole Black Forest. The lake was created in the bowl of a former glacier, and although it has are no fish, the water being too poor in oxygen, legend has it that there are a few water-sprites living in it.

Famous writers such as Grimmelshausen and Mörike have described gnomes and water-sprites as living here. It was believed to be fathomless, and woven around with saga and fable, until in 1738 a more literal-minded soul measured the depth and found it was only 20 metres.

In Unterstmatt, a popular ski-ing region on the ridge of the Black Forest, one can be carried up on a ski-lift to the Hornisgrinde, 1164 metres high. Swabians use the term Grind to describe the head or the skull, which exactly fits the round, bare shape of this panorama hill.

Ski-lifts are also available up the Mehliskopf, which with its 1008 metres altitude also counts as a reliably snowy area. Summertime enjoyment is also available not far from the car-park of the Kurhaus Sand, as the Schwarzenbach reservoir is only a short hike away. When its dam was completed in 1926 it was the highest in Germany. One can walk along the top of it, which is 380 metres long, and watch the wind-surfers sailing on the 70 hectare surface of the reservoir.

The viewing tower on the 1003-metre high Badener Höhe is also easily reached from Kurhaus Sand. At its feet lies the little Herrenwieser See. From the cross-roads near the hotel one can drive down hill to Bühl, to the home of Bühl damsons, a delight particularly in spring or when the damsons are being harvested. There is a drop of 600 metres on these 20 kilometres of road, and in spring-time one often travels from snow down into the first of the blossom.

One can tell that the cosmopolitan spa town of Baden-Baden is not far away when one sees, on a hill above the pass, the **Bühlerhöhe** Hotel, a remote luxury hotel in one of the higher price brackets. The rich widow of an army general created it as a convalescent home for army officers; it was not until much later that it became a hotel for the highest ranks from the worlds of politics and big business.

A fine view from a magnificent position - the Bühlerhöhe luxury hotel

The journey now continues in the direction of Geroldsau, where one can turn off a short distance to see the Geroldsau water-falls before finally reaching the end of the Black Forest High Road, Lichtental, and the cosmopolitan spa town of Baden-Baden.

4. Northern Black Forest
4.2 Baden-Baden

This world-famous spa town on the banks of the River Oos obviously has something that other spa towns lack. Is it the casino, that tempts the rich and the beautiful to settle down in Baden-Baden? Is it the race-course and the equine sports that draws High Society? Or is it the enjoyable mixture of hot springs and Black Forest landscape that exercises this irresistible charm?

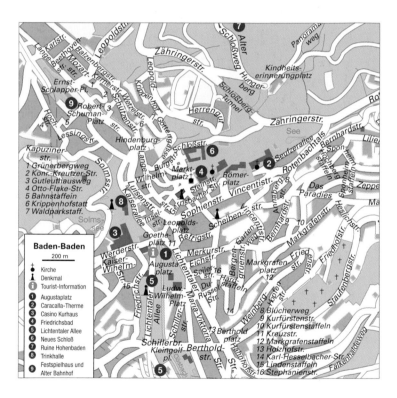

Baden-Baden is acclaimed as one of the most elegant hot-spring spa towns in Germany, and it has also built up a name for itself as a location for business conferences and political meetings.

The Roman Emperor Caracalla used to visit these baths, seeking relief from his rheumatism. The Counts of Baden made the town their residence in the 12th century, and in the 16th century

Paracelsus, one of the founders of modern medicine, treated his patients here.

The town still to this day retains its importance as a luxurious spa town. The historic Friedrichsbad (1877) stands in Marktplatz (the main entrance is in Römerplatz), and these Roman-Irish baths are regarded as one of the finest examples of spa culture.
The Caracalla leisure baths are altogether younger and more modern, and one of the most beautiful hot-springs baths in the Black Forest. Marble goddesses gaze down on the lively hurly-burly below the gigantic dome of the baths. Anyone who swims out into the open-air pool can enjoy the back-drop of the town of Baden.

The Caracalla leisure baths in Baden-Baden

The Romans discovered and used the first brine baths, and even today nearly a million litres of this hot water bubble out of the ground every day - up to 70°C hot, and a cornucopia for the town that has always given it a certain touch of luxury. Underneath Römerplatz, Roman baths have been excavated and here one can see the earliest example of hot-water heating.

The history of the spa town comes to life at a number of points. Next to the Kurpark is the old Kurhaus, and inside is the **casino,** a magical point of attraction for all visitors. The gaming rooms and the ballrooms and concert halls disseminate a luxuriant, cosmopolitan atmosphere such as one finds in the great hotels in the town.

The luxurious atmosphere in the gaming-room in Baden-Baden

The Kurhaus is a building in the neo-classical style, designed by Friedrich Weinbrenner, who also endowed the fan-shaped city of Karlsruhe with its late-classical features. Since 1855 there have been four luxuriously appointed gaming rooms in the right-hand wing of the building, designed in the style of the French royal palaces. The nearby "pump room" (1842) is decorated with wall frescoes on which one can find figures and scenes taken from Baden legends.

One can also trace the 2,000-year history of the town in the municipal museum, "Im Baldreit". Porcelain from the municipal "manufactory", which existed between 1771 and 1778, is also on dis-

The spa hall also contains the casino

The Festspielhaus, one of Europe's greatest opera and concert houses

play here alongside objects of daily use and archaeological documentation. From the **Neues Schloss** on the Florentinerberg, which also contains a collection of municipal history, one can enjoy an incomparable view of the town and the convent church. Count Ludwig Wilhelm, who ruled Baden from 1677 to 1707 and has gone down in history as "Türkenlouis", found his last resting-place here in the Choir. The convent of Lichtental lies at the end of Lichtentaler Allee, one of the most beautiful prome-

Opening times
"Im Baldreit" municipal museum

Tuesday to Saturday,
10.00 am to 12.30 pm
and 2.00 to 5.00 pm

Municipal History Collection
1st April to 30th September

Tuesday to Saturday,
10.00 am to 12.30 pm
and 2.00 to 5.00 pm

nades in the town. It is the oldest such building still preserved in Baden, and is still today a Cistercian nunnery. It would be wrong to leave the town without having also seen something of the surrounding area, for instance by travelling by mountain railway to the top of the Merkur (868 metres) to enjoy a fine view, or on foot

to the **Altes Schloss Hohenbaden,** built by the Counts of Baden but relinquished as their residence at the end of the 15th century in favour of the Neues Schloss. Not far away is the Battert, a steep formation of cliffs and the remnant of a Celtic ring fort. A short excursion can be made to the castle of **Ebersteinburg,** which offers a delightful view and a restaurant within the castle walls. The castle ruins of Yburg lie some six kilometres south of Baden-Baden, in the midst of vineyards. Anyone who clambers the 110 steps to the top of the tower will be rewarded with a magnificent view across the Rhine plain to the Vosges.

Another fine piece of architecture, which most people from Baden-Baden see at some time or other, stands directly alongside the motorway and is much younger; the pyramid-shaped structure of the motorway church (1978) was created by the architect Friedrich Zwingmann and the painter and sculptor Emil Wachter. At first glance it is a rather plain structure of concrete, glass, and slate, but the interior is bright and warm.

The exciting high-point of a visit to Baden-Baden is a visit to the race-course, where in the spring and the autumn the International Club holds its Iffezheim Race Weeks. No-one needs to be afraid of coming into contact with the highest of high society; the race meetings offer all the fun of the fair, for old and young. Fine ladies in huge hats are only usually to be found on the reserved seats of the Club grandstand, and betting and participation in the great event are open to everyone.

Entrance costs very little, and one can make the round of the presentation ring, where the horses are displayed, to the betting window, the race track, and the winner's platform as many times as one likes, until time and betting-money have run out.

4. Northern Black Forest
4.3 Rastatt, Gernsbach, Murgtal

Rastatt's baroque magnificence makes a delightful contrast to the wonders of Nature to be enjoyed in a drive through the Murgtal, which opens out onto the Rhine plain here. Count Ludwig Wilhelm of Baden, also known as "Türkenlouis", had ordered Rastatt to be converted into a fully fortified city after transferring his residence here from Baden-Baden, and as part of this programme he also had the palace built here at the end of the 17th century.

The gigantic, three-winged palace, built of coloured sandstone, is set in a beautiful park and contains the Ancestors' Hall as the central point in the Princes' living quarters. Stucco figures represent Turkish prisoners, ceilings and walls all luxuriantly decorated.

Adjoining it to the south is the baroque palace church of the Holy Cross, planned by Michael Ludwig Rohrer and dating from 1723. Its interior contains an impressive High Altar and a ceiling painting depicting the legend of the Holy Cross. The weaponry museum gives an outline of German military history on the ground floor of the main building. The Federal Archives have also set up a memorial to the freedom movement in German history.

Opening times for the Rastatt Palace

**Only in conjunction with conducted tours
Tuesday to Sunday, every hour,
10.00 am to 4.00 pm
but 1st April to 31st October, until 5.00 pm**

**The Palace church is on
account of recovering closed**

The Einsiedler chapel at the far end of Kapellenstrasse completes the group with the park and the water-organ in the town centre. The Pagodenburg, a polygonal pavilion, lies in the midst of extensive terraced gardens which start just behind the chapel

The palace and gardens of Rastatt lie in the middle of the town

The palace is inextricably linked with the history of the old town. Separated from the palace by the market square, the town hall dates from 1750 an is also a Rohrer design. The symmetrical building also includes the Johannes Nepomuk fountain and the Alexius fountain.

Türkenlouis' widow, Countess Sibylla Augusta, also built a luxurious summer residence, the Schloss Favorite, five kilometres south of Rastatt between the villages of Forch and Kuppenheim. It was built at the beginning of the 18th century, and was in those days in the depths of the countryside, some way away from the town.

The Sala terrena, the reception and ceremonial hall, lies in the centre of the palace and stretches up through two storeys with a cupola dome above it. The interior furnishings are particularly luxuriant, and reflect the Countess' enthusiasm for ceramic work.

The magnificent reception rooms possess costly inlay floors. The Hall of Mirrors and the Florentine Room represent the ultimate criteria for the artistic craftsmanship of the times, as does the collection of porcelain on the second floor.

Gaggenau, at the entrance to the Murgtal, is the business and shopping centre for the valley. The modern thermal and mineral baths in the Bad Rotenfels district make a charming contrast to the commercial hurly-burly of the town itself.

In **Gernsbach,** which has held municipal rights for more than 750 years, the lovely old town centre is well preserved; the 17th-century town hall stands on the left bank of the Murg, its gables decorated with spirals and lacy tips. Schloss Eberstein lies a little further up the valley, on the road to Baden-Baden, and offers a fine view into the valley.

The Counts of Eberstein lived here from the middle of the 13th century until 1660. The castle was completely rebuilt at the end of the 18th century, and in 1950 the ruin of the castle keep was also restored.

The landmark of Forbach is the roofed wooden bridge, dating from the 16th century. It is the longest single-span wooden bridge in Europe. This little town is a very suitable starting-point for excurs-ions up the valley, which becomes ever narrower and ever more unspoilt and is a fine area for hiking and biking.

The **Schwarzenbach dam** is easy to reach from here, as are the higher levels either side of the Black Forest High Road. A typical feature of the upper Murgtal is the little hay-huts perched on the steep meadows, which even nowadays still have to be mown by hand.

The old original Black Forest, such as Wilhelm Hauff described in his story "The Cold Heart", can still be enjoyed to the full in Raumünzach and Schönmünzach. The story is set in the days when thick pine trunks still used to be floated down the Murg.

4. Northern Black Forest
4.4 Karlsruhe, Bad Herrenalb, Frauenalb, Albtal

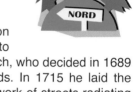

Karlsruhe is known as the "fan-city" on account of the fan-shaped layout given to it by Count Karl-Wilhelm of Baden-Durlach, who decided in 1689 to build a palace on his hunting grounds. In 1715 he laid the foundation stone for the fan-shaped network of streets radiating outwards from an octagonal tower which grew into a city during the 19th century.

Friedrich Weinbrenner, an architect who himself came from Karlsruhe, gave the city its late-gothic appearance. This was the period during which the market square and the town hall were built, and a small pyramid containing the grave of the founder of the city can still be seen in the centre of this metropolis of Baden.

The spirit of rivalry between Baden people and Swabians is proverbial, particularly since the Swabians have provided Stuttgart as the State capital. However, the "fan-city" does not need to be afraid of any competition; it now boasts Germany's second biggest inland port and a university that originated from Germany's oldest seat of higher education.

The palace still marks the centre of the city, although only the small octagonal tower is left from the original version. The new buildings arose in the second half of the 18th century, under Count Karl Friedrich. The exterior was faithfully restored after the palace had been destroyed in the second world war. The palace nowadays houses the Baden State Museum, with major collections dating from antiquity and showing the history of art and culture from the Middle Ages to the present day. The visitor can also see the famous collection of Turkish trophies amassed by Count Ludwig Wilhelm of Baden, known as "Türkenlouis". The modern parts of the collection, from art nouveau to the applied art of the present day, are on display in the Museum.

The State Natural History Museum has a permanent exhibition of local and exotic flora and fauna in life-like dioramas and biological groups. Stones, minerals, and fossils provide information about the creation of the Earth and the diversity and development of life.

The State Art Gallery is regarded as the most significant museum of art in southern Germany. It houses not only a major collection of paintings by German Old Masters but also many works by the Black Forest painter Hans Thoma.

The Karlsruhe Centre for the Arts and Media Technology may still be young, but it already enjoys an international reputation. The public is invited to participate actively, with exciting interactive installations. The museum was opened in 1997 and possesses one of the largest media-art collections in the world, including a number of classics from this new world of "media art". Video-sculptures are just as much represented here as the painting, sculpture, and photography of the past 25 years.

Opening times Karlsruhe Palace
Mon. closed, Tue., Thur., Fri., 10.00 am to
5.00 pm, Wed., 10.00 to 8.00 pm, Sat. and
Sun., 10.00 to 6.00 pm

Museum beim Markt Every day except
Monday 10.00 am to 5.00 pm
(but Wednesdays 1.30 to 8.00 pm)

State Natural History Museum
Tuesday to Saturday, 10.00 am to 4.00 pm
Sunday, 10.00 am to 6.00 pm

State Art Gallery
Tuesday to Friday, 10.00 am to 5.00 pm
Saturday, Sunday, and public holidays,
10.00 am to 6.00 pm

Centre for Art and Media Technology
Lorenzstrasse 19; Wednesday to Saturday,
12.00 noon to 8.00 pm
Sunday, 10.00 am to 6.00 pm

Karlsruhe people have always been aware of their close links with the Black Forest, but it was not until the tram route was built from the centre through the Albtal to **Bad Herrenalb** that they have had this recreational area virtually outside their front doors.

Baden people have nurtured their reputation for technical ingenuity by coming up with the clever idea of letting their trams run on ordinary railway tracks.

It is thus possible to travel up the Albtal either in the modern manner, in a tram running to a set timetable, or stylishly and nostalgically in one of the steam trains that often run at weekends. The first stop on this route should be Ettlingen. The town on the edge of the Black Forest has a palace that once belonged to Countess Sybilla Augusta of Baden where nowadays the well known palace festival is held before the magnificent backdrop of the Court of Honour. The palace also houses the Ettlingen muni-

The entrance to the spa park of Bad Herrenalb

cipal museum, which is in fact four museums: the Albgau Museum shows the history of the Ettlingen region from the early Stone Age to the 20th century; the Karl Albikert Museum is dedicated to this sculptor (1878 to 1961) and his works; the Karl Hofer Museum exhibits the oil paintings and drawings of this painter (1878 to 1955); and the Museum of East Asian Art is a branch of the Linden museum in Stuttgart. The Motor Museum in Marxzell contains more than 300 motor vehicles and a collection of old tools, motor-cycles, and bicycles, as well as railway exhibits from the age of steam. It is dedicated to Carl Benz (of Daimler-Benz fame), whose family came from the nearby village of Pfaffenrot, and was established in 1968 by private initiative.

Another nearby village contains a famous landmark of the Albtal, the renovated baroque convent church of Frauenalb. Peter Thumb, the architect from the Vorarlberg, drew up the plans for

Opening times
Albgaumuseum
Karl Albiker Museum
Karl Hofer Museum
Museum of East Asian Art
Tuesday to Sunday, 10.00 am to 5.00 pm

Marxzell Motor Museum
Every day, 2.00 to 5.00 pm

this church, and it was built in 1727. There is no mistaking its similarity with the twin towers of the monastery in St Peter, which was also designed by Peter Thumb. Frauenalb used to have an allied monastery in Bad Herrenalb, likewise endowed by the Eberstein dynasty in 1149.

The Cistercian convent of St Maria, at the mouth of the Albtal, where seven little Schwarzwald valleys run together, is now in the middle of the smart spa town with its thermal baths and spa gardens. A magnificent old tree now grows out of the ruins. The most important work of art in the church is the monument to Count Bernhard of Baden on the north wall of the Choir.

Bad Herrenalb has been a popular thermal spa town since the

beginning of the 20th century. With its winter-sports area and numerous hiking paths, it has become a popular starting-off point for excursions, for instance to the Poltzsägmühle, a saw-mill more than 700 years old. In the centre of Bad Herrenalb one can also make an excursion back into one's own childhood, or even into that of one's parents and grandparents, because the Toy Museum shows how life was lived in the past on the basis of old dolls'-houses.

"Paradise", a remnant of the Herrenalb monastery

4. Northern Black Forest
4.5 Pforzheim, Wildbad, Enztal

Pforzheim is also known as the city of gold, and as the gateway to the Black Forest, holding the latter title because it stands at the confluence of the Enz, the Nagold, and the Kleiner Würm. Even the Romans appreciated this means of access, settled here, and gave it the name of portus - "gateway". It nestles under the Schlossberg, and is also the birthplace of the great humanist Johannes Reuchlin. It was totally destroyed in the last war, and today the town's long history is only reflected in the restored castle and monastery church of St Michael, originally dating from 1230 AD, and a few other remnants.

Count Karl Friedrich of Baden laid the foundation stone in 1767

Pforzheim, a city famous for its goldsmiths and the gateway to the Black Forest

for the jewellery industry that today still dominates the town when he built the "manufactory for clocks and fine steel wares", and the visitor can trace this history in the Jewellery Museum in the Reuchlin house. This shows items of jewellery from the past five millennia as well as pieces that mark out the development of the local industry. Jewellery history also plays its part in the Technical Museum of the Pforzheim Jewellery and Clock-Making Industry (at Bleichstrasse 81), a visit to which is a worthwhile addition. The town centre of Pforzheim is dominated by the style of the Rebuilding Age; the main railway station with its glass reception hall dates from 1957, and the main post office and the town hall, with its carillon of bells, also date from this period. Unspoilt Nature starts immediately where the town ends. The bank of the Enz was once the site of the State Garden Show, and has now

Opening times Jewellery Museum
Tuesday to Sunday, 10.00 am to 5.00 pm
Different opening times on public holidays
Tel. 0 72 31/ 39 21 26, Fax 0 72 31/ 39 14 41

Technical Museum of the Pforzheim
Jewellery and Clock-Making Industry
Wednesday, 9.00 am to 12.00 noon
and 3.00 to 6.00 pm
Every 2nd and 4th Sunday in the month,
10.00 am to 5.00 pm

returned to the condition favoured by nature conservationists, a long strip of gardens with water-organs and playgrounds. Thanks to a very attractive water playground it is of interest to young and old, amateur architects and boatmen alike.

Enz, Nagold, and Würm flow together here

Further attractive and easily reachable excursion destinations on the edge of the Black Forest include the monastery of Maulbronn, which is listed as part of the World Cultural Heritage, and the little village of Tiefenbronn, south-east of Pforzheim. The Tiefenbronn Altar and the Magdalene Altar (1431) by Lucas Moser stand in the parish church of St Mary Magdalene. Pforzheim marks the start of the Westweg, probably the best-known long-distance hiking path in Baden-Württemberg, which leads via all the most beautiful and the highest viewing-points in the Black Forest and ends in Basle after a hike of more than 280 kilometres. In

Neuenbürg one can re-live the history of mining in the Black Forest; the Frischglück mining museum leads deep into the mountains around the Enz, far below the peak on which the old castle towers over the valley. Long ago, Celts and Romans used to dig out the iron ore from here.Wanderkilometern in Basel.

Calmbach is the confluence of the Kleiner Enz and the Grosse Enz, and **Bad Wildbad** is an old spa town in the Grosser Enztal. According to an old legend, which is also illustrated by a mural in the spa hotel, the thermal springs were discovered by a duck who entered the warm water seeking relief from painful injuries. It was an aristocratic spa town at the turn of the century, as the restored princes' spa baths in the Palais Thermal show. Whilst one can enjoy the very gentle climate down in the Enztal, one can also take the mountain railway to the top of the Sommerberg and enjoy a still mild but rather more bracing climate. Hiking paths lead from here to the mountain marshes of Wildsee and Hohlohsee.If one drives further up the Grosser Enztal in the

Bad Wildbad, at the foot of the Sommerberg - its main attraction it its thermal baths

direction of Freudenstadt, one comes to the source of the Enz and to a particular attraction at Enzklösterle; the quiet Poppelsee invites every visitor for a walk round its bank, and in the holiday season one can also see a charcoal kiln at work. In the village of Poppeltal one can slide down into the valley on a giant stainless steel slide.

4. Northern Black Forest
4.6 Calw, Nagold, Nagoldtal

The twists and bends of the **Nagoldtal** between Pforzheim and the main town of Nagold represent the natural frontier between the Black Forest to the west and the Swabian plateau to the east. The hills and slopes become steeper and higher as soon as one leaves Pforzheim. In Bad Liebenzell one can climb to the castle ruins high above the valley and look down into this healthy thermal spa town, the name of which is derived from that of St Lioba.

Nestling under the castle ruins - the town centre of Bad Liebenzell in the valley of the Nagold

The castle was built in the 12th century by the Counts of Calw, and today houses an international youth centre and youth hostel. The Benedictine monastery in Hirsau was built even longer ago, in 830 AD, and although today only parts of it are preserved the size of its ground give an indication of its size.

The elms that once grew out of the ruins, and to which the poet Uhland once dedicated a poem, have long since disappeared, but the monastery walls have still lost nothing of their mysterious attraction.

The elegant Owls' Tower is still preserved from the original monastery complex, together with the four-sided cloister and St Mary's chapel, now an evangelical church. A museum has been set up in its upper floor containing finds relating to the monastery's history. The monastery museum documents the history of the monastery in a large number of displays.

In **Calw** there are still many reminders of the town's most famous son, Hermann Hesse. A fountain bears his name, and a museum in the Vischer-Schütz house illustrates the main stages in his life. Calw was founded in 1037 by the Counts of Calw, and later gained great significance through the salt trade and later the timber trade.

Opening times Monastery Museum

April - Oct., Tuesday to Sunday 2.00 to 5.00 pm
Nov. - March, Saturday & Sunday 2.00 to 5.00 pm

Hermann Hesse Museum, Marktplatz 30

Tuesday to Sunday, 2.00 to 5.00 pm
Thursday till 7.00 pm Sunday, 11.00 am to 5.00 pm

The fine half-timbered houses in the old town centre form an almost complete historical collection around the market square. The gothic chapel of St Nikolaus stands on the medieval Nagold bridge.

In spring every year, the crocus meadow below the ruined castle of Zavelstein turns into a sea of petals. This village stands on a promontory above the Teinachtal. The castle keep at the end of the old village street provides a fine view, and is a last remnant of a Roman-style castle dating from the first half of the 13th century.

Right in the middle of **Bad Teinach** there is a modern spa building next to the historical spa hotel and baths, which date from 1842, including the "pump room" and the spa administration. Not far away one can find the mineral springs, and can go in and look round by prior appointment.

The little town of Wildberg is in an exposed position, high above the Nagold valley. The upper town lies in a very regularly shaped bend in the Nagold, and every two years is the venue of a traditional village festival, the Schäferlauf. This dates back to 1443, when the shepherd gained respectability by founding a guild in Markgröningen on the Neckar. This brought them their own court of law, the Schäferlauf procession, and a shepherds' dance. In 1723, Duke Ebeerhard Ludwig of Württemberg made Wildberg the venue for the meeting of shepherds from all over the northern and central Black Forest.

In front of the town hall, with its vaulted alley entrance, there is a market fountain dating from 1554, and at the other end of the mountain ridge the walls of the ruined castle are still preserved. The Wildberg museum is in a former fruit barn belonging to the Reuthin monastery. It exhibits agricultural implements, and gives an insight into the history of the town.

Opening times for the Wildberg Museum

All year round Sunday and public holidays 11.00 am to 5.00 pm

Nagold is a town of half-timbered houses and the main town in its valley

Nagold, the main town in the valley, occupies a broad riverside meadow. It was first mentioned in historical records in 786 AD. Its display-piece is the historical Alte Post hotel, a half-timbered building 300 years old with a fine wrought-iron sign hanging out at the front. The parish church of the evangelical Remigius congregation is also worth seeing; it stands on the cemetery site, and was first mentioned in historical records in 773 AD. Towering above the little town is the ruined 11th-century castle of Hohennagold.

5. The German Clocks Road

The German Clocks Road in the Black Forest was inaugurated in 1992. Following four years of planning and preparation, a holiday road had been created that aroused enormous interest with visitors to the region. It follows a snaking course for more than 320 kilo-
metres north-westwards from Villingen-Schwenningen and back, passing through all the most beautiful Black Forest valleys on the way.

It connects more than 30 different places, and gives and impression of the significance of clocks from the Black Forest, originally made of wood, in the development of crafts and industry, and thus in the economic development of the whole region.

Cuckoo-clocks are just as much part of the Black Forest as the red-bobbled Bollenhut or Black Forest cherry cake. No other kind of craftsmanship so personifies the character of the region's people and landscape. Making the best out of existing resources, with great skill and hard work, called for endurance and ingenuity. Black Forest wooden clocks, of which there are of course many different kinds, with or without cuckoo, have now become synonymous all over the world for the Black Forest.

The region has been producing and selling cuckoo-clocks for more than 250 years, with growing success. This is the reason why one hears the cuckoo out of doors far less often than from inside the wooden case of a clock.

Black Forest people did not actually invent the clock; they only constructed it with the means at their disposal. Skilled craftsmen were able to produce the first wheel-driven clocks without any initial training. There was also no guild of clock-makers; anyone who was able to construct one was able to call himself a master-craftsman.

The clock-making trade developed quickly; many people in the meagre mountain farm business had only a meagre income, and were looking for gainful employment. And many of the wealthy families in the towns were only able to buy a clock, from 1750 onwards, because these started to become available at an affordable price.

It is believed that one Franz Ketterer, from Schönwald, built the first cuckoo-clock in 1730. A papal legate, after having visited the monastery of St Blasien in 1762, mentioned "the wooden clocks that are made here in great quantities, and have been disseminated by trade throughout Europe". By the end of the 18th century it is believed that 110,000 such clocks had were being produced every year, and 600,000 by 1854.

The Black Forest clock merchants had branch offices on four continents and in 23 countries as long ago as 1840. In China and Russia, in Turkey and America, the little wooden bird was opening his window every hour on the hour to "call the time".

The facets of Black Forest wooden clocks are as diverse as the region itself. The original form of drive was a heavy stone fastened by a cord to the wooden gears.

The mechanism was sometimes made of iron or brass, but always mounted in a wooden housing. The wood for the face and the hands could be obtained from the immediate vicinity, but the gears had to be made from hard orchard wood, which grew at lower levels.

Standing clocks are amongst the most beautiful the Black Forest produces. Even now, the fine wooden cases are produced by cottage industry or sometimes in artists' workshops. Painted cases dominated until the middle of the 19th century, but then gave way to the unstoppable advance of cuckoo clocks.

In many cases, the little house from which the cuckoo emerges every hour is modelled on the country railway stations of the day. The foundation stone for this success was laid by the engineer, Robert Gerwig, who built the Black Forest Railway. He had arranged a competition for the most beautiful and most typical clock housing. A professor of architecture from Karlsruhe, Friedrich Eisenlohr, won the competition with a clock construction that looked like one of the small trackside buildings of the day. There is a simple reason for the fact that the cuckoo always looks out from just under the roof. Its call consists of only two notes and is relatively easy to imitate; it also sounds very harmonious. A specialist firm in Schonach supplies 150 different kinds of cuckoo call, although there are more than 800 different types of cuckoo clock. Although the market for clocks and watches has changed very rapidly, the cuckoo clock still remains firmly under German control. Cheap "Made in Taiwan" imitations of Black Forest clocks do not sell anything like so well. On the contrary, the trend is more towards the bigger, hand-built clocks with complicated clockwork mechanisms. However, it is no longer possible to attain the unit volume of cuckoo clocks of a hundred years ago; it is estimated that 350,000 are produced annually. On the other hand, the clock-making industry that has now superseded the craft was by 1989 already producing about 60 million clocks, watches, and mechanisms annually, and thus employing about 12,000 people.

The history of clock-making in the Black Forest can be traced by following the Clocks Road from Villingen-Schwenningen. The Franciscan Museum in Villingen, and the Clocks Museum and Clock-Making Industry Museums in Schwenningen make a good start. Clocks and watches are still produced here by Kienzle and Schmeckenbach, but only sold in small quantities through jewellery shops. The route is marked by brown road-signs with the wording "Deutsche Uhrenstrasse", and first leads towards Furtwangen. One passes through Unterkirnach and reaches Vöhrenbach, where the Uhrmache-rhäusle ("clock-maker's cottage") stands. Eisenbach, on the highest part of the Black Forest, not far from Titisee, is the next stopping-point; there is a collection of clocks in the reading-room of the Wolfwinkelhalle, and Johann Baptist Beha's "world clock" ticks in the Hotel Bad.

The visitor will find more information about the history of clock-making in the Heimatstube of the spa town of Neustadt. The Höness clock factory produces original Black Forest cuckoo-clocks and standing clocks. From Neustadt, the Clocks Road runs in a great loop through Lenzkirch, where one can see

Gutachtal

Schwarzwald
haus

Scho

Trib

Tennenbach-Kapelle
Emmendingen

Waldkirch

Benediktiner-
kloster
St. Peter

Furtw

Glottertal

Hex
mül

St. Märgen

Freiburg

Feldberg

Höllental

Hinter-
zarten   Titisee

Benediktinerkloster
St. Trudpert-Münstertal

DEUTSCHE UHRENSTRASSE

Lauterbach

Schramberg

nberg

Rottweil

h

St. Georgen

Deißlingen

jen

Trossingen

Villingen-
Schwenningen

Bad
Dürrheim

ch-

Schloß
Donaueschingen

HENSTRASSE

Eisenbach

Deutsche
Uhrenstraße

see-
stadt

luchsee

various old clocks in the Zunft- und Heimatstube. The road then runs along the bank of the Titisee and on into the Langenord-nachtal. Two kilometres further on, one turns off towards the Schottenhof, were a type of clock called the Schottenührle is produced. The valley also contains Waldau, where the Kreuz brothers constructed the Black Forest's first wooden balance clock in the middle of the 17th century. At the Thurner cross-roads the Clock Road leads off in the direction of St Märgen and St Peter, and this stretch of the Road offers the most beautiful landscape. St Peter offers a baroque organ clock in the monastery church. Passing the turn-off towards the Kandel, the road leads down into the picturesque Glottertal, where the television series "Black Forest Clinic" was filmed. Where the valley leads out onto the Rhine plain, the Clocks Road turns of to the right into Elztal. In the Elztal Museum in Waldkirch one can see beautiful musical clocks by Ignaz Bruder and an extensive organ department. The Road then leads through Kollnau and Gutach and on through the Elztal to Bleibach, where the Simonswald valley turns off.

Many clock-makers used to work in the long stretched-out village of Simonswald, and clocks are still made there today. The landscape of the valley appears to be quite untouched, with fine farmhouses looking down from the slopes at the Wilder Gutach. The road through the valley is 18 kilometres long, ending in steep upward hairpin bends to Gütenbach, which like Neukirch is one of the "birthplaces" of clock-making. IIn Gütenbach, the village museum exhibits large-scale clock mechanisms and a church-tower clock by the Gütenbach master, Philipp Furt-wängler. Not far away, in Furtwangen - one of the most important stopping-points on the Clocks Road - there used to be the first school of clock-making and wood-carving.

The College of Advanced Technology in the town teaches precision engineering, electronics, and information technology, and thus provides to-morrow's clock-makers with state-of-the-art technology. The German Clocks Museum stands alongside the College and boasts more than 4,000 exhibits. As documentation of the history of the clock-maker's art and as a collection of Black Forest clocks it is regarded as the most comprehensive of its kind anywhere.

This journey through time now follows the B500 main road to Schönwald. In Kehren one can drive up onto the plateau, and spend a few sunny hours as if in the peace and quiet of the 18th century. A flourishing craft trade has developed here since Franz Ketterer produced the first cuckoo-clock. Some firms are still producing cuckoo-clock in Schonach, Triberg, and Hornberg, the next stops along the Road. Here in the Gutachtal one is surrounded on all sides by clocks, in shops, factories, and workshops. The Black Forest Clock Museum in Triberg also presents a collection of the finest examples. In the clock tower of the town hall in Hornberg the bells are driven by clockwork. The Clocks Road leaves the Gutachtal at this point and winds steeply up the Reichenbachtal, thr-ough Lauterbach, and then down into the valley again. The standing clock in the old town hall is well worth seeing.

Down in the Schiltach the Clocks Road finally reaches Schramberg, still a major centre of the clock-making industry. An astronomical clocks chimes the hours from the town hall. The firm of Junghans produces clocks for the world market, but sells them only through the specialist trade. The Road then goes further via Tennenbronn to St Georgen, on the high plateau of the Baar. Clock-makers and sellers originally clustered around the monastery, an important feature in those days, and on this basis there later developed a gramophone industry which was in turn superseded by the electronics industry.

There is a Museum of Clocks, Watches, and Gramophones in the town hall displaying old clocks and tools. In Peterzell the Road leaves the B33 trunk road and swings away towards Königsfeld. The village museum in Buchenberg houses a regional exhibition of clocks and clock-making.

The Lauber clock factory is the sole remaining manufacturer of original painted-case clocks. The Clocks Road, which is always well signposted, now leads to Niedereschach, where the mechanism of a church-tower clock is on display in the town hall, and then to the neighbouring village of Horgen. The sun-dial mounted on a block of stone is not a work of mechanical art, but has still kept the time precisely for centuries. Rottweil, the oldest town in Baden-Württemberg, also has a clock-making history. The Minster of the Holy Cross has a sun-dial, and there is a coat-of-arms in the town hall where a baroque clock can be seen.

The firm of KB-Uhren exhibits unique clocks such as miniature road clocks. The clockwise circuit is now complete; leaving the old town centre of Rottweil by the B27 trunk road one comes to Deisslingen, where there is a beautiful standing clock in the first floor of the town hall. Although Trossingen has made more of a national name for itself with musical instruments, it also used to be an important centre of the clock-making art.

The museum of local arts and crafts exhibits old clocks and clock faces from the Black Forest, and the Selva-Technik clock factory supplies spare parts and components for amateur clock-makers, including complete kits. Weigheim-Mühlhausen, where fine wall-clocks can be seen in the Heimatstube, is the last stopping-place on this tour before the visitor travels back through the spa town of Bad Dürrheim to the double city of Villingen-Schwenningen.

Wood carvers in the Black Forest have plenty of work when the Fasnet season

6. Tips for hikers

6.1 Plattensee, Zweribachfälle

6.2 Freiburg Schauinsland

6.3 Between Kinzig- and Elztal:
    from Hofstetten to Biereck

6.4 Black Forest High Road
    Bühlertal

6.5 Northern Black Forest:
    Kaltenbronn - Hohlohsee

Hiking through the Black Forest must be the oldest original way of enjoying this landscape. Thanks to the lively help of the Black Forest Association, one will find well signposted hiking paths in almost every town and village.

The great long-distance hiking paths stretch out over the forests and mountains like a net. The famous Westweg, from Pforzheim to Basle, for instance, is the hiker's "royal road".

The best-known sights and viewing-points are strung out one after another along a distance of 280 kilometres. Hornisgrinde and the Mummelsee are only two examples of points to be reached in a hike lasting nearly two weeks, and which simply must include the Feldberg and the Belchen.

Anyone who would like to take things a little more quietly should choose one of the shorter and less strenuous mountain paths such as the Mittelweg, from Pforzheim to Waldshut (230 kilometres in nine days), or the Ostweg from Pforzheim to Schaffhausen (240 kilometres in ten days). One must allow at least five days for the Kandel-Höhenweg from Oberkirch to Freiburg, and the Gäurandweg takes four days from Mühlacker to Schopfloch.

A special pleasure for wine-lovers: the Ortenau Wine Path is a series of routes one can also cover without luggage, or the Markgräfler Wiiwegli, either of which will require three days. There also very many cross-routes enabling the hiker to make up any journey he or she likes.

The tourist information office in each town and village has of course also prepared routes and tours which are well signposted and easy to follow. Finally, there is also a large number of hiking guide-books and maps to help hikers find their way. More and more villages and hotels also offer "hiking without luggage" facilities, meaning that the overnight luggage is delivered during the day to the next destination.

6.1 Plattensee, Zweribachfälle

This hike starts from a point high above St Peter. From the village itself one crosses the St Märgen road, drives across the so-called Potsdamer Platz, and goes on to the Plattensee and parks the car.

The hiker leaves the Plattensee off to the right, and soon comes to the Lanackerhof. Blue diamond-shapes mark the way to the Zweribachfällen, leading steeply downwards to the foot of this waterfall.

The next series of signs to follow are a black dot on a yellow background. The path leads steeply up-hill in the direction of Hohwartsfelsen, and after a total walking time of an hour and a half one is again at an altitude of 900 metres.

The viewing-point offers a fine view of the Wilder Gutach and the Zweribach valleys. The path then leads back, half-right at the next fork, still following the signs with the black dot, into the Bannwald forest.

After a total walking time of 2,5 hours, we turn off to the left and following the signs with the green dot. Only a few minutes later we turn off to the right and come, after a total of 2,5 hours, to the road at the Plattensee.

6.2 Freiburg Schauinsland

Anyone who would like to start off on a short excursion from Freiburg into the Schwarzwald mountains has one obvious choice: Schauinsland is this city's own private mountain. Leave the car behind, and travel by public transport to the station at the bottom of the Schauinslandbahn, which will swing you quickly up to an altitude of more than 1200 metres.

After getting out, it is best to take a short walk to the viewing tower or to the Schniederli Museum. Returning to the top station one can follow the path running parallel to the road, crossing it about 10 minutes later.

There is a large car-park on this side of the road, followed by a path signposted with a red dot on a white ground. About a quarter of an hour later, the hiker leaves the forest and looks down into the Münstertal. The Giesshübel restaurant is a welcome opportunity to rest and recover for a moment before crossing the road and walking further.

From the next cross-roads one follows the path marked with a blue diamond-shape and a figure "1". A walk of about two hours takes one to the Eduardshöhe, and then follows the signs further to Holzschlägermatte, passing the Lehhof.

The path through the forest leads down-hill, and we can soon start to follow the signs to the bottom station. After a total of 3 hours we are back at the starting-off point of our hike.

6.3 Between Kinzig- und Elztal:
From Hofstetten to Biereck

Hofstetten, the starting-off point for this hike, can be reached where the road branches off at the entrance to Haslach. The car can be parked in the town centre, in front of the town hall. Unterdorfstrasse leads off to the right from the main road and then on in the direction of the Fehrenbacherhof.
The signposts consist of two intersecting diagonal red bars. Ten minutes later, at the entrance to the village, a small tarred road

leads up- and one reaches the Fehrenbacherhof after a total of three-quarters of an hour.

We then encounter the Hansjakobweg, signposted with a black hat on a white background. After an hour and a half we reach Heidenstein, where there is an illustrated signboard, and ten minutes later at a cross-roads we follow the signs consisting of a "5" and a green cross.

Reaching the Palmenhöhe, we come onto the Lahr-Rottweil path which brings us to the Rössel at Biereck (the signposts are a red and yellow diamond-shape); this is an idyllic and very historical tavern, where the Schellenmarkt is held every Whitsun: it used to be a market for shepherd-boys to buy and sell bells for their sheep.
One follows a short stretch of road from here, and then a well marked hill path branches off to the left and leads into the

The joys of hiking and fine views at all times of the year

Kinzigtal. After another 20 minutes one reaches the Brosemenshof, and is back at Hofstetten after a total of nearly four hours.

6.4 Black Forest High Road Bühlertal

The Schwanenwasen restaurant is only a few kilometres south of Baden-Baden, on the Black Forest High Road, and makes a good starting-point for a hike below the Bühlerhöhe, a hill and a hotel full of tradition.

The car can be left behind at the restaurant while one first follows a narrow road signposted "27" and leading slightly down-hill. After a quarter of an hour, one leaves a right-hand bend by turning off to the left and follows the signposts for about 45 minutes to the "Kohlbergwiese", originally quarters for building workers on the Bühlerhöhe project and now a friendly tavern with a view of the luxury hotel.

One now follows the "28" signposts and those pointing towards "Brockenfelssattel-Hertahütte". At a fork in the path one goes straight ahead (signposted "Bühlertal"), and after nearly an hour reaches the Brockenfelshütte, and then a bend to the left, and then the fine view from the Hertahütte.

One can then go a short way back along this narrow path and follow the signposts to "Bühlertal" again, until after a total of an hour an a half one finally sees a sign, "Plättig", and can return to the Black Forest High Road. At the entrance to the Bühlerhöhe hospital there is a path to the left, the Philosophenweg, which leads back to Schwanenwasen.

6.5 Northern Black Forest: Kaltenbronn - Hohlohsee

Kaltenbronn lies below the highest point of the pass between the Enztal and the Murgtal, which one goes through on the way from Bad Wildbad to Gaggenau.

The car should be parked in car-park C at Schwarzmiss, at the top of the pass, so that one can walk along the right-hand edge of the car-park onto a path signposted with a "2", reaching the Hohlohturm in only ten minutes. It was built in 1897 as the Kaiser Wilhelm tower to provide a fine, distant view.

Relaxation high above the Black Forest valleys

One can now follow the "2" signs back, turning off to the left to reach the nature-conservancy area of Hohlohsee, marching along over railway sleepers across the marshy ground, and reaching the lake after a total of 30 minutes.

This upland marsh is covered in a typically Nordic vegetation, with birches and woolly grass. The path now bends to the left and follows the Mittelweg (Pforzheim to Waldshut), marked by a red diamond-shape with a white bar across it.

After three-quarters of an hour one reaches the Hotel Sarbacher at the edge of Kaltenbronn, crosses the road, and follows the path with the green "4" signs to the Kreuzlehütte. Here we turn off after an hour and a half onto the Westweg, marked with a red diamond-shape on a white background, which leads us back to the Schwarzmiss after a total of two hours.

7. Wintersports

A perfect winter - the higher levels of the Black Forest offer just that, if the weather is kind to us. Even in less snowy years, these higher levels above 1000 metres often have sufficient snow cover, and the local communities - and of course the winter-sports enthusiasts - have long become accustomed to good conditions being available in these southern German mountains for the "white sport".

However, the Black Forest is the ski-er's natural home for a different reason as well: the first Alpine ski club was founded in Todtnau, more than 100 years ago.

The number of ski-runs has since risen rapidly, and more and more ski resorts are trying to provide constantly good facilities with flood-lights and snow-cannon. Snowboarders are also using the ski-runs in front of their own front doors for surfing on the white waves.

However, anyone who restricts his or her winter sports to Alpine ski-ing is missing much that is on offer. The resorts and the ski-ing clubs have long developed a spider's web of Loipen - cross-country ski routes - all across the Black Forest uplands.

One can make a silent tour over the snow around one's own ski resort, and there are also long-distance Loipen just as there are long-distance hiking paths

The centres of Alpine skiing in the Black Forest are Todtnauberg, Muggenbrunn, and Fahl, with 21 ski-lifts of various kinds and 50 kilometres of prepared ski-runs back down into the valley. The southern Black Forest has a total of more than 100 ski-lifts serving ski-runs mainly of ordinary to average levels of difficulty and heights of more than 1400 metres. And of course there are on the Feldberg extensive tour routes for cross-country skiers; after all, this is the home of the German national centre for com-

petitive skiing at Herzogenhorn, where the professionals train. However, most cross-country skiers prefer the heights around St Peter and St Märgen, or make their grooves in the snow of the Notschrei Loipe on the Schauinsland or on the Stübenwasen. Many also use the Loipe centre at the Thurner for longer runs, or set off from Hinterzarten - this town can be reached easily by train.

The cross-country skiing centre at Belchen-Hohthann was one of the first of its kind, and is an attractive starting-point and finishing-point for the Schonach-Belchen long-distance skiing route. At its far end is the Loipen area around Martinskapelle, north of Furtwangen and the Brend, which can be reached from Schonach. Another centre for Alpine skiing is the Black Forest High Road. To either side of the 60-kilometre stretch between and Freudenstadt, all along the ridge of the Black Forest, there are sufficient lifts and Loipen for

Fun of winter sports can be guaranteed on the highest mountain in the Black Forest

both skiers to enjoy both kinds of the sport. One can rely fairly well on sufficient snow in this part of the central Black Forest, as it lies at altitudes between 900 and 1100 metres.

In the northern Black Forest, on the other hand, Alpine skiing is not nearly so important as cross-country skiing. At Kaltenbronn, and also at the Dobel, although higher altitudes are attained, the 1,000 kilometres or so of ski paths and Loipen tend to be more popular. Freudenstadt alone boasts 120 kilometres of marked Loipen, and from the hill just outside Wildbad, the Sommerberg, one can ski all across the plateau to Kaltenbronn.

Whereas in January and February cross-country skiers tussle for victory in the Rucksack-lauf or the Black Forest Skiing Marathon, amateurs can also try out long-distance skiing. The skiing path runs from Schonach to the Belchen and is 100 kilometres long. In the northern Black Forest the skiin-path consists of a number of sections between

Alpirsbach in the south and Dobel in the north. Three smaller long-distance routes lead from the Thurner to Hinterzarten and from there to the Schluchsee or the Belchen. Anyone who does not actually strap on a pair of skis can certainly enjoy watching skiing, particularly the more spectacular kinds - which are not quite as dangerous as they look. Ski-jumps are mainly to be found in the major winter-sports resorts such as Hinterzarten or Peterstal-Griesbach. And, because skiers cannot quite do without their sport even in the summer, summer ski-jumping often takes place in the warmer months.

Another attraction for spectators is sledding races. These wooden monsters with which loads used to be brought down to the valley in days gone by are now usually handled by two drivers, and more for sports purposes. A quieter kind of enjoyment is available on the toboggan runs, where one can enjoy the pleasures of winter sports with very little risk of injury. The one at Todtnau is 3.5 kilometres long, and must be the longest of its kind in the Black Forest. Natural and artificial skating-rinks in many resorts offer the possibility of turning a few artistic circles, and when the Titisee freezes over it offers one of the most beautiful of these natural rinks. Anyone who prefers a touch of the romantic should take a ride in a horse-sleigh, wrapped in warm blankets and accompanied by the bright clatter of the harness bells. In St Peter, for instance, one can be towed through the snowy winter forest behind a breed of horse called a Black Forest Fuchsen.

Dog-sled races are just one of the events in the winter calendar

8 Special Events

The calendar of special events in the Black Forest is full to the edges. There is a rich programme of events in every month to dispel any threat of boredom. Once the rockets have all been fired off on New Year's Eve it is time to start on the revelries of Fasnet. From schmutziger Dunschtig - the Thursday before the start of Lent - to Ash Wednesday, the Alemannic Fasnet (or Carnival) season flourishes briefly but wildly. The strongholds of this tradition are Donaueschingen, Villingen, Schramberg, Gengenbach, the Elztal, and Rottweil.

After all these wild fun and games, a week later there is Scheibenschlagen, a sport involving hurling glowing discs of wood into the valley to start bonfires. Easter festivities in the Black Forest are accompanied by artistic craftsmanship, and in many places there are exhibitions showing the various techniques used and the original Easter decorations.

There is a procession of shepherd in traditional costume in Bad Peterstal-Griesbach in April, and that is when the jazz festival starts in Villingen.

May is the month in which the wine festivals start on the Upper Rhine and the Kaiserstuhl. In Iffezheim, near Baden-Baden, there is the Spring Meeting, an international (horse)-racing week.

The festival in Ettlingen starts in June, as it does at a number of open-air theatres, and on the Biereck near Hofstetten there is the Schellenmarkt at Whitsun. Many towns and villages celebrate Corpus Christi in this month with elaborate processions, carpets of flowers decorate the streets, and the locals dress up in their finest traditional costume. The processions in St Peter, the Glottertal, and Bad Peterstal are particularly well worth seeing. Freudenstadt has a town festival, the festival starts in Gengenbach and in Freiburg the Tent Music Festival.

In July one can watch the "Hornberg Cannonade" being re-enacted, and the concert season starts in Rastatt. There are summernights' festivals in Titisee-Neustadt and on the banks of the Schluchsee.
The Kinzig raft-harbour festival is held in Wolfach in August, and there are grand firework displays by the waterfall in Triberg, at the mansion in Staufenberg, and at the castle in Durbach.

A festival is held in the castle of Ortenberg, near Offenburg, and the Laurentius festival for shepherds and farmers is held on the Feldberg. Baden-Baden organises a town and baths festival, and in Emmendingen the Breisgau Wine Festival starts with the coronation of the Breisgau Wine Princess.

In September one should make time for the Oechsle festival in Pforzheim and for race-days at Iffezheim, near Baden-Baden. This is the month in which the Damson Festival starts in Bühl, the town festival in Rottweil, and the Ortenau Wine Festival in Offenburg. There are also wine festivals in many places on the Kaiserstuhl and the Rhine valley.

There are still many wine festivals going on in October: the Baden Wine Market in Offenburg, and the Achkarrer Wine Days and the Autumn Wine Festival in Oberbergen, to mention just a few. There is even a Horseradish Festival in Appenweier-Urloffen, and by way of complete contrast the Donaueschingen Music Festival for contemporary music.

St Katharine's Day is celebrated with fairs and markets in November, for instance in Sasbach, and St Martin's Day with fairs in Haslach and Gengenbach.

More and more places are holding highly original Christmas markets in December, one of the biggest and finest of them being in Freiburg.

There is a Christmas crib competition in Schenkenzell, and many towns have New Year's Eve concerts, such as the one in the Villingen Minster. A tour through the Black Forest as a training course in wines and the joys of the table would be just the right way to enjoy all these treats at once.

9 Daytrips

There is no excuse for boredom when one visits the Black Forest, but anyone who has to make a long journey to get here should also look round at the many attractive day trips which one can so easily make from here.

It is really only a stone's throw to Lake Constance, also known as the Swabian Sea. The A81 motorway will simply take you further south and you will soon be in Constance or Meersburg, and can leave the car and transfer to one of the ships of the White Fleet.

On the Rhine side of the Black Forest, the A5 motorway takes you in less than an hour from Freiburg to Basle, and it is well worth visiting Switzerland and seeing the enchanting town centre of Basle. Then there is the Basler Zolli, the fantastic zoo on the other side of the Rhine.

The Upper Rhine, between Waldshut and Schaffhausen, exerts a charm of its own. The landscape between the Hotzenwald and the Swiss Jura is gentle and charming, and the accent even on the German side sounds very much like Swiss German. No-one would want to miss a visit to the Rhine waterfall at Schaffhausen, where huge masses of water roar and crash down into the depths.

Right on the border to the Black Forest there is a special kind of magnet

Meersburg on Lake Constance is only a stone's throw away

that draws huge crowds. North of the Kaiserstuhl, one can leave the motorway at Ettenheim and Herbolzheim and drive directly to one of the biggest and most beautiful leisure parks in Germany:

the Europa-Park was created by the Waldkirch family of Mack, who run their cheerful and adventurous business all over the world.

The Kaiserstuhl itself is still often counted as part of the Black Forest, but its mild climate and the dominance of wine-growing is almost an island of the Mediterranean in the midst of the Rhine plain. The best way of exploring the volcanic outcrop is on foot, or with a bicycle. Wine-lovers are overcome with delight at the names of all the great vintners and wines that come from here. A circular tour is just the right way of undergoing a training course in wines and enjoying the pleasure of the table.

Bridges across the Rhine give access to the attractions of our neighbours: Colmar can be reached in just a few minutes from Freiburg or Breisach. The French style of life and smart wine-making villages make Alsace an attractive alternative to the Black Forest and the Rhine plain. There is a Wine Road on this side of the Rhine as well, with its highest point at the Route des Crêtes forming the counterpart to the Black Forest High Road.

Strasbourg is one of the great international cities of Europe. From Offenburg one drives to Kehl and then over the Rhine directly into the city, and can visit the Minster and the European Parliament, or even "Little Venice", the old town centre on the banks of the river.

To the north, Heidelberg is a fixed item on any tourist's list. It is a university town on the banks of the Neckar with a beautiful ruined castle on the hill above and a picturesque town centre which has retained a flair of its own despite the large number of visitors.

The other well known student town of Tübingen offers an enchanting contrast and a supplementary programme to a tour of the Black Forest. Why not spend a day with the students, in the lecture rooms or punting, instead of in monasteries or romantic steam trains? This typically Swabian town has so often been the home of writers and philosophers, and offers a medieval town centre and a great deal more besides.

The Swabian's heart also beats faster at the name of Ulm. As a bastion on the border to Bavaria, this former imperial city has developed into the commercial and cultural centre of its region. The Minster at Ulm, on the banks of the Danube, and the fine gothic town hall are well worth visiting.

The Minster in Ulm links the Middle Ages with our own times.

Schwarzwäld

Gutacher Tracht

Fronleichnamsprozession

Schnapsbrenner

Strohschumacherin

Uhrenschildmaler

Räucherkammer

INDEX

MUSEUMS

CASTLES

Edm. von König Bildarchiv

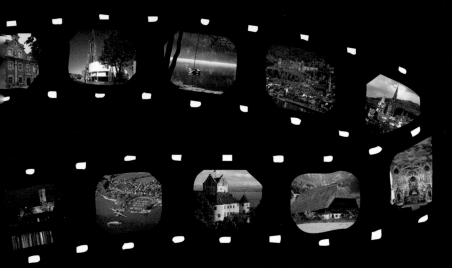

Fotografien nationaler Sehenswürdigkeiten, Panoramen, Kirchen, Schlösser und Burgen bis hin zu Luftaufnahmen. Besonders geeignet für Hotel- und Gastronomiebetriebe sowie der Reise und Touristikbranche. Dieses und viel mehr können wir Ihnen für Ihre bildunterstützte Gestaltung von Werbebroschüren, Flyern uvm. anbieten.
Nutzen Sie unser immer größer werdendes digitales Bildarchiv zu fairen Preisen. Wir freuen uns über Ihre Anfrage.

Edm. von König Creativ

Hier entfaltet "der König" für Sie seine ganze Creativität. Ob individuelle Gestaltung Ihrer Firmenbroschüre, Hauspostkarte, Hotelprospekte, Geschäftsausstattung oder Entwurf eines Signets oder Logos. Edm. von König Creativ wird Ihnen königliche Gestaltungen präsentieren.

KUNSTVERLAG GmbH & Co KG

1882
Edm. von König

www.verlag-koenig.de

Schillerstraße 48 · 69234 Dielheim · Postfach 1027 · 69232 Dielheim · Telefon 0 62 22 / 98 16 - 0

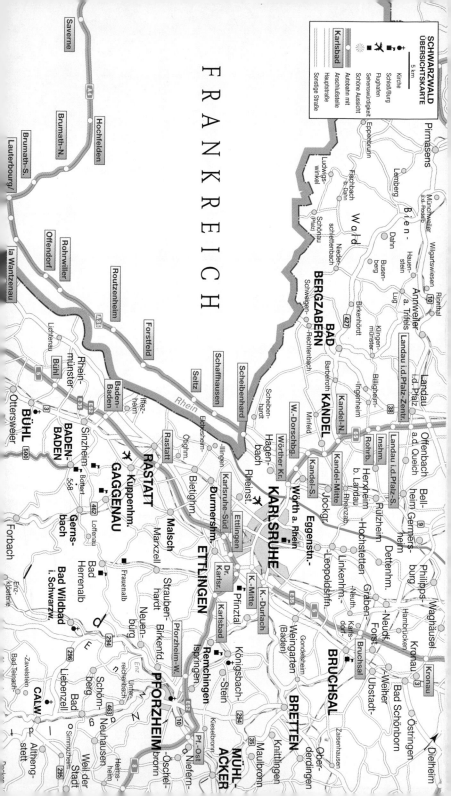

SCHWARZWALD ÜBERSICHTSKARTE

Kirche
Schloß/Burg
Flughafen
Sehenswürdigkeit
Schöne Aussicht
Autobahn mit
Anschlußstelle
Hauptstraße
Sonstige Straße

Karlsbad

5 km

FRANKREICH

Pfälzerwald – Bienwald

Saverne
Pirmasens
Münchweiler a.d. Rodalb
Wilgartswiesen
Rinnthal
Hochfelden
Lemberg
Hauenstein
Annweiler a. Trifels
Landau i.d. Pfalz
Brumath-N.
Dahn
Busenberg
Lug
Brumath-S.
Ludwigs-winkel
Schönau (Pfalz)
Niederschlettenbach
Birkenhördt
BAD BERGZABERN
Lauterbourg/
Fischbach b. Dahn
Eppenbrunn
Schweigen-Rechtenbach
Klingenmünster
BAD BERGZABERN
(427)
la Wantzenau
Offendorf
Rohrwiller
Routzenheim
Barbelroth
Ingenheim
Billigheim-
KANDEL
Landau i.d. Pfalz-Zentr.
Landau i.d. Pfalz-S.
Offenbach a.d. Queich
Bell-heim
Germers-heim
Philipps-burg
Forstfeld
Schaffhausen
Scheibenhard
Rhein
Minfeld
Kandel-N.
Rohrb.
Insh.
Herxheim b. Landau
Hochstetten
Rheinzab.
Dettenhm.
Waghäusel
Hambrücker
Kronau
Dielheim
Lichtenau
Rhein-münster
Bühl
Baden-Baden
Iffez-heim
Scheiben-hardt
W.-Dorschbg.
Wörther Kr.
Kandel-S.
Kandel-Mitte
Eggenstein-Leopoldshfn.
Graben-Neud.
Kronau (3)
Otterswei
BÜHL (500)
BADEN-BADEN
Ötigheim
Illingen
Ötigheim
Elchesheim-
Rheinst.
Hägenbach
WÖRTH A. RHEIN
Linkenhm.-
Neuth.
Karls-dorf
Neudf.
Forst
Bad Schönborn
Ötringen
Forbach
Sinzheim
Bottert 568
Rastatt
Bietighm.
Karlsruhe-Süd
Jockgr.
KARLSRUHE
B
Ubstadt-Weiher
(3)
RASTATT
Kuppenhm.
GAGGENAU
(462)
Loffenau
Malsch
Marxzell
Durmersheim
Ettlingen
K.-Mitte
Gondelsheim
Weingarten (Baden)
BRUCHSAL
BRETTEN
(35)
Gerns-bach
Bad Herrenalb
Frauenalb
Strauben-hardt
ETTLINGEN
Dr. Karls.
Prinztal
K.-Durlach
Weingarten (Baden)
Bruchsal
Knittlingen
Maulbronn
Bad Wildbad i. Schwarzw.
Neuen-bürg
Birkenfd.
Karlsbad
Pforzheim-W
Königsbach-Stein
Kieselbronn
Oberderdingen
Zaisenhausen
Enz-Klöterle
(294)
(296)
Schöm-berg
Unterreichenbach
Remchingen
Ispringen
(294)
MÜHL-ACKER
Bad Teinach
Zavelstein
Bad Liebenzell
CALW
Schöm-berg
Neuhausen
PFORZHEIM
(463)
(10)
Pf.-Ost
Niefern-Öschel-bronn
Heims-heim
Althengstett
Simmozheim
Weil der Stadt
(295)
(8)
Altheng-stett